Creating a
HERB
GARDEN

Creating a
HERB
GARDEN

Designing, planting and growing – a practical guide

Jessica Houdret

Special photography by Andrea Jones

southwater

To Jeremy

This edition is published by Southwater

Distributed in the UK by
The Manning Partnership
251-253 London Road East
Batheaston
Bath BA1 7RL
UK
tel. (0044) 01225 852 727
fax (0044) 01225 852 852

Distributed in Australia by
Sandstone Publishing
Unit 1, 360 Norton Street
Leichhardt
New South Wales 2040
Australia
tel. (0061) 2 9560 7888
fax (0061) 2 9560 7488

Distributed in New Zealand by
Five Mile Press NZ
PO Box 33-1071
Takapuna
Auckland 9
New Zealand
tel. (0064) 9 4444 144
fax (0064) 9 4444 518

Southwater is an imprint of
Anness Publishing Limited

© 2000
Anness Publishing Limited

1 3 5 7 9 10 8 6 4 2

Publisher: Joanna Lorenz
Senior Editor: Doreen Palamartschuk
Designers: Ruth Hope and Lilian Lindblom
Special photography: Andrea Jones
Illustrator: Madeleine David

Previously published as part of a larger book *The Ultimate Book of
Herbs and Herb Gardening*

p.1: *A group of herbs, including clary sage and Jacob's ladder against a wall.*
p.2: *Red and white valerian contrast with the blue of cornflower.*
p.3: *A colourful herb display with fennel in the foreground.* **Above:** *Elderberries
and bergamot.* p.6: *A selection of containers suitable for herbs.*
p.7: *A planted-up herb pot.*

Contents

Introduction

Herbs are a diverse and versatile body of plants, which have been appreciated through the centuries for their many uses. In the past they were the main source of raw materials for medicines, nutritional supplements and culinary flavourings as well as fulfilling a wide variety of household needs. They provided fragrance in the home, were added to bath and beauty preparations, used as dyes, cleaning agents, insect repellents and other similar products which we have become used to buying ready made.

Although few people now would presumably want to give up the benefits of modern medical science or the convenience of contemporary technology and goods, there is an increasing revival of interest in herbs and their uses, which has been gathering momentum since the 1980s. Alternative therapies and herbal healing have gained ground and many more people add herbs to their cooking as a matter of course. This may be partly due to a current inclination towards natural products and natural practices, and partly due to increased travel and communications, which have brought the cuisines and ingredients of the world before a wider audience.

In addition, in more recent times, a new element has emerged: herbs have gained respectability. They are no longer seen as solely the preserve of eccentrics, nor are herbal remedies universally dismissed as superstitious nonsense. The reason is that much traditional herbal folklore has been vindicated by modern research. Scientific studies have proved that many herbs have antibacterial, antifungal, antidepressant and other medicinal properties and that some help to lower blood pressure or act on the hormonal systems of the body. Many plants are now recognized by the medical establishment as providing the key to discovering new drugs to combat the major modern illnesses such as cancers and AIDS.

Growing your own herbs is immensely rewarding, with the added advantage of having fresh material to hand, for use in home remedies and recipes, which you know has not been sprayed, adulterated or polluted. This book contains background history, ideas for schemes and layouts and a section on growing herbs and making the most of these useful plants in an ornamental setting. In the section on using herbs, you can find out how to harvest, store and preserve herbs, how to make oils and tinctures, and reap the benefit of creating your own herb garden. Not only are herbs objects of academic study, they are also living plants, scented, exuberant and colourful – there to grow, to use and, above all, to enjoy.

Jessica Houdret

History of Herbs

The first question explored here is what is meant by the term "herb"? This is followed by some guidelines on restrictions in using these powerful plants and a detailed explanation of plant classification, how it began and developed, and the helpfulness of using Latin names to avoid confusion. A background history of herbal knowledge and use through the centuries comes next. The chapter concludes with a summary of some of the landmarks in herbal literature.

Above *A topiary spiral emphasizes the symmetry of the raised stone urns in a small formal herb garden.*

Left *An arched walkway shelters raised beds, thickly planted with herbs, in a reconstruction of a medieval cloister garden.*

What is a Herb?

The definition of the term "herb" has varied over the centuries. At one time it meant primarily grass, green crops and leafy plants. This concept entered into many dictionaries, where the definition was narrowed to a plant that does not have a woody, persistent stem, but dies down to the ground after flowering – a herbaceous plant, in other words. This was clearly inadequate, because it excluded some of the most obvious and common herbal examples such as rosemary, thyme and sage.

A herb is now generally understood to mean a plant, some part of which, roots, stem, leaves, flowers or fruits, is used for food, medicine, flavouring or scent. This wide category covers much more than a few plants with small green leaves; and includes some trees, shrubs, sub-shrubs or woody-stemmed perennials. Annuals, even ferns and fungi, as well as the herbaceous group, could also fit the general description.

Right *Watermint and bogbean in a pond.*

Below *A detailed illustration of St John's wort,* Hypericum perforatum, *from W. Curtis's* Flora Londinensis, *1826.*

Most of the plants included in this book have a long herbal history, their therapeutic uses having been recorded in early manuscripts or published works written by the specialists of the time. Some of these uses seem very far-fetched or downright dangerous in the light of modern knowledge. Expressed in colourfully poetic language, the early records often deal with bizarre conditions and unfamiliar illnesses, from attacks by "flying venom" and "elf-shot" to agues, fluxes and St Anthony's fire – as well as coughs, fevers and more recognizable medical problems.

However, the remarkable fact is that many herbs have been found under modern analysis to vindicate our fore-fathers' faith in them. Recent research studies have established the antibacterial, antiseptic, anti-inflammatory or other medicinal properties of large numbers of common herbs.

Herb chemistry is very complex. Each individual variety of plant is unique in its make-up, even closely related species are quite distinct. They all contain many active constituents which work together to affect the functions of the body, when used for medicinal purposes. This holistic (or synergistic) method of using the whole plant, as opposed to taking a concentrated extract, is the gentlest and safest way to benefit from herbs.

Aconitum napellus, *or monkshood (top), and* Atropa belladonna, *deadly nightshade (above), are highly toxic in any quantity.* Cannabis sativa *(right) is one of the plants subject to legal restrictions in most countries.*

Restrictions on Herbs

Safety in use

Many plants are highly toxic and can be dangerous in use. Self-medication is not advised and it is always best to seek the advice of a qualified medical practitioner before herbs are used as a treatment. Plants can look very similar and common names are often misleading – there is a danger of mistaking one herb for another. Before collecting a herb, ensure that it has been correctly identified and do not interchange similar species for a particular purpose, as they may not have the same properties.

It is also essential to use only the part specified, usually the leaf, stem, flower or seed and occasionally root. Some plants classified as herbs are highly poisonous in any form or quantity, monkshood, *Aconitum napellus*, being an example. It should be remembered that many apparently benevolent substances, for example vitamins, can be toxic if taken to excess. This principle applies to herbs too and includes the common culinary ones, such as thyme or rosemary. It is difficult to ingest a harmful amount in the form of the whole leaf, and most are totally safe if used, fresh or dried, in the quantities recommended in recipes. However, in the form of essential oils, which are concentrated extracts of the active principle, they can be highly toxic.

Legal restrictions

There are legal restrictions both on the use or trade and on the collection or cultivation of various herbs. Restrictions also cover certain herbal extracts and preparations, and their permitted concentrations and doses, as well as those people allowed to administer, prescribe or supply them.

Growing herbs that are capable of producing illegal drugs, or cultivating species considered to be noxious weeds, is against the law in some countries. It is also a criminal offence to collect or uproot wild plants that are protected by law.

Plant Names

Herbs are listed in this book under their Latin, or botanical, names. This helps to avoid confusion, as most have several common names which vary according to country, or even from one local region to another. Sometimes the common name used in one country refers to a totally different plant in another country. The Latin names have the advantage of being international. *The International Code of Botanical Nomenclature*, set every five years following an international conference, ensures that all countries accept the same botanical names.

In recent years, however, there has been a spate of reclassifications of plants by botanists in the light of new studies or detailed analysis of specimens. For example, the plant always known as *Mentha rotundifolia* var. 'Bowles', (or Bowles' mint), has now become *Mentha* x *villosa* f. *alopecuroides*. As far as possible the most current name is listed, but changes are ongoing.

Common Names

The most usual common name is also given in this book, along with variations and synonyms where applicable. Both Latin and common names are often a lively indication of a herb's history, properties or use.

Above *Cultivars of* Achillea millefolium.

Plant Classification

The system of plant classification by Latin names in use today was developed by Carl Linnaeus, 1707–1778, a Swedish botanist and professor of medicine at Uppsala University, near Stockholm. He divided plants into groups, according to common characteristics.

Some modifications have since been introduced, but the system remains essentially the same as at its inception. Under the Linnaeus system all plants have a double name. The first is the name of the genus, or wider grouping, to which they belong, and the second denotes their individual species. Generic names, like all Latin names, are either masculine, feminine or neuter.

Thus *Achillea* = genus, *millefolium* = species. The second part of the name also indicates whether a plant is a hybrid or cultivar, or has been subdivided, according to finer differences, as a subspecies, variety or form.

Plant Divisions

FAMILY – A group of plants, made up of a number of genera with characteristics in common, usually decided by the structure of flowers, fruits or seeds e.g., ROSACEAE. Some families have alternative names, such as COMPOSITAE also known as ASTERACEAE. The first is the traditional name, which, although it remains valid at present, is being superseded by a newer name, designed to fit into a standardized system of nomenclature, whereby all family names end with "aceae", preceded by the key genus of the family, as ASTER-ACEAE.

GENUS – A group, made up of a number of related species, such as *Achillea*, but which may also contain only one species, such as *Anethum graveolens* (denoted by the first part of the Latin name).

SPECIES (spp.) – Individual plants that are alike and breed naturally with each other, such as *Achillea millefolium* (the species is denoted by the second part of the Latin name).

HYBRID – A cross between two species, or genera, indicated by a cross, such as *Lavandula* x *intermedia*.

CULTIVAR – A variant of the species or hybrid that has a special characteristic, such as leaf variegation, developed and maintained under cultivation. For instance, *Melissa officinalis* 'All Gold', a golden-leafed lemon balm. The name of the cultivar is printed in roman type, within inverted commas (single quotation marks).

VARIETY (var.) – A subdivision of species and hybrids, often with a distinctive difference (such as flower or foliage colour), but with only minor variations in botanical structure, such as *Lavandula dentata* var. *candicans*.

SUBSPECIES (subsp.) – A variant of a species, such as *Lavandula stoechas* subsp. *pedunculata*.

FORM (f.) – Has only minor, but often noticeable, variations from the species, such as flower colour, e.g. *Lavandula stoechas* f. *leucantha* – a white-flowering form of *L. stoechas*. (Note that, once a genus has been stated, it can then, as here, be represented by its initial.)

System of plant classification

LABIATAE/LAMIACEAE

FAMILY

Mentha

GENUS

Lavandula

GENUS

Achillea

GENUS

L. stoechas

SPECIES

L. latifolia

SPECIES

L. angustifolia

SPECIES

L. dentata

SPECIES

L. dentata
var. *candicans*

VARIETY

L. stoechas
f. *leucantha*

FORM

L. stoechas
subsp. *pedunculata*

SUBSPECIES

L. angustifolia
'Hidcote'

CULTIVAR

L. angustifolia
'Munstead'

CULTIVAR

L. x *intermedia*

HYBRID

L. x *intermedia*
'Grappenhall'

CULTIVAR

L. x *intermedia*
'Seal'

CULTIVAR

Herbs in History

There is ample evidence of the herbal use of plants by the civilizations of ancient Egypt, over a period from 3000 BC to the reign of Cleopatra, which began in 48 BC. Papyri dating from 2800 BC record the medicinal use of some familiar herbs, including juniper, mint and marjoram. The wall paintings of tombs and temples reveal the use of aromatic plants, spices and gums in religious and funerary rites and on social occasions. Also an inscription in the temple of Karnak relates Ramses III's plea to the god Amun for victory in battle, reminding him of the pharaoh's generous sacrifice of 30,000 oxen, quantities of "sweet-smelling herbs and the finest perfume". Archaeologists have also found the physical remains of plants, flowers and seeds used for food and flavouring, as votive garlands and in cosmetic and embalming ointments.

Offerings made to the sun god Ra, at Heliopolis, included a concoction of 16 herbs and resins. Known as *kyphi* or *khepri*, it was adopted by the Greeks, and then the Romans, and was described by Dioscorides. Later analysis confirmed that it contained among its ingredients *Acorus calamus*, cassia, cinnamon, peppermint, juniper, acacia and henna.

The Greeks, the great period of whose culture overlapped with the end of the Egyptian dynasties, adopted Egyptian skills in making ointments from aromatic plants, as their literature often confirms. The cosmetic use of plants was a frequently described theme:

He really bathes
In a large gilded tub, and steeps his feet
And legs in rich Egyptian unguents;
His jaw and breasts he rubs with thick
palm oil,
And both his arms with extract of
sweet mint;
His eyebrows and his hair with
marjoram,
His knees and neck with essence of
ground thyme.
– Antiphanes

Above *Plants being ground in a mortar, from a 10th-century French herbal.*

The Romans have left many records of their use of herbs for flavouring food, in perfumery, for decoration and strewing at social events. Medicinal uses are discussed in the works of writers such as Pliny. The vast spread of their empire also meant that the Romans took Mediterranean plants to northern areas that had never known them before and where many became naturalized.

After the fall of Rome, in the period sometimes known as the Dark Ages, AD 476–c.1000, herbal knowledge was nurtured and kept alive in Christian monasteries. In Britain during this time, Anglo-Saxon writings show a wide knowledge of herbs and evidence of correspondence with centres in Europe.

The Eastern Connection

During the 10th century a great Muslim empire stretched from the eastern Mediterranean, taking in Arabia, Persia, parts of Spain and North Africa. Arab academics were paramount in the medicinal practice of the time and Avicenna, born in Persia, AD 980, was one of the most famous. He was the first to describe the making of attar of roses by distillation, was instrumental in the discovery of plant essential oils, and his *Canon* became a standard medical text. Crusaders from Britain, who set out to destroy the Muslim influence, brought home the new plants and exotic spices from the Near East.

Above *A relief at the Temple of Karnak in Luxor, Egypt, depicting a botanical garden showing plants brought from Syria by Pharaoh Tutmosis III.*

In India, where so many medicinal and scented plants grow, there is a long tradition of using spices and aromatic herbs in cookery, for perfumes and cosmetics. An 18th-century Italian traveller wrote that "nowhere do the women pay greater attention to their cleanliness than in the East, bathing frequently and massaging all parts of their body with perfumed oils". Ayurvedic medicine, practised in India, is an ancient system based on herbs and shares many similarities of concept with Chinese herbal medicine, whose longest unbroken tradition of practice is often considered to be the most ancient in origin. The Yellow Emperor, Huang Ti, born *c.* 2000 BC, wrote a medical treatise which is often cited as the earliest herbal on record. Chinese herbalism is currently enjoying a revival in the West.

The Renaissance and the Discovery of the New World

With the Renaissance, the great revival of learning marking the birth of modern Europe, came advances in medicine and the study of the healing properties of plants. The 16th and 17th centuries were the age of great herbalists and herbals: Turner, Gerard and Parkinson in Britain; Brunfels, Fuchs and Bock in Germany; Clusius, L'Obel and Dodoens in the Netherlands; Mattioli and Porta in Italy.

Above *A man and woman harvesting sap, from* Le Livre des Simples Médecines, *a 15th-century French herbal.*

Above *Collecting herbs to use in the stillroom.* Spring *by Lucas van Valkenborch, 1595.*

At the same time the use of herbs in cookery, perfumery and for cosmetics was widespread and well documented in many books on household skills, such as Sir Hugh Platt's *Delights for Ladies*, 1594, and T. Dawson's *The Good Housewife's Jewel*, 1585. It should be remembered, however, that the line between perfumery for pleasure and health was a narrow one. It was generally accepted that a fragrant smell was in itself proof against infection and many recipes in the stillroom books for perfumed powders and pot-pourris, which would now be considered fripperies, had a serious underlying purpose.

In the 16th and 17th centuries a huge quantity of new plants, many of which were used by the Native Americans in their traditional medicine, were brought to Europe from the Americas. Seeds were taken the opposite way by the early colonists keen to establish, in their new country, gardens stocked with the familiar herbs of home – including parsley, savory and thyme.

The Modern Era

Up until the 18th century, botany and medicine were closely allied, but with the rise of modern scientific enquiry they drew apart as separate disciplines. During the 19th century the medical establishment turned away from plant-based remedies, and synthetic drugs, produced in the laboratory, began their ascendancy. This is not to say that old herbal remedies and culinary and cosmetic recipes disappeared: traditions were kept alive in many country districts and in some countries never fell from use. In Europe the day-to-day use of herbs remained more widely practised than it did in Britain.

Mrs Grieve, whose famous herbal was published in 1931, did much to promote the renewed interest in herbs in Britain in the 20th century, as did Eleanour Sinclair Rohde, who wrote many books on herbs and became a popular lecturer on the subject in the United States, following World War II.

In the latter part of the 20th century the revival of interest in all things herbal continues. Emigration and accessibility of travel have spread the use of culinary herbs and spices across many countries and cultures. There is wide recognition among scientists today of the value of plants as the basis for drugs to combat major diseases, such as cancer and AIDS, and much research is being carried out. However, the drugs under development depend on isolating and copying active plant compounds. This takes a different direction from the use of the whole plant as practised in traditional herbal medicine.

Old Herbals

Old herbal manuscripts make fascinating reading. They give an insight into how herbs were used in the past and increase our general understanding of the subject. Not all are readily available and are kept in specialist libraries, but some have been reissued in modern editions and facsimiles and many are widely quoted from by modern authors. The following are some of the more important works on herbs written in the West.

Early Manuscript Herbals

c. 320 BC *Historia Plantarum* and *De Causis Plantarum* – by Theophrastus, *c.* 370–286 BC, Greek philosopher and pupil of Aristotle. (Edited and translated as *The History of Plants* and *The Causes of Plants* by Sir A.F. Hort, Loeb Library, 1916.)

c. AD 60 *De Materia Medica* – written by Dioscorides, a Greek physician, living in Rome. Describes 600 herbs and their healing properties. It became the standard work on medicine, influencing most herbals that followed for over 1,500 years. (English translation by John Goodyer, 1655.)

c. AD 77 *Naturalis Historia* – by Pliny the Elder, contemporary of Dioscorides. A massive, 37-volume work, 16 concern trees, plants and medicines.

AD 400 *The Herbal of Apuleius* – Author unknown. Originally written in Latin it drew quite heavily on Dioscorides and Pliny, adding pagan prayers and superstitions. It was much copied over the years. (Anglo-Saxon translation made in 11th century.)

c. AD 900 *The Leech Book of Bald* – compiled by a Saxon physician. Reveals a wide knowledge of native plants and includes prescriptions sent by the Patriarch of Jerusalem to King Alfred.

c. 1150 *Physica* – by Hildegard of Bingen. Unique as a book on the medicinal properties of plants by a woman and had great influence on the famous German "fathers of botany", Brunfels, Fuchs and Hieronymus Bock.

c. 1248–1260 *De Proprietatibus Rerum* by Bartholomaeus Anglicus, an Englishman living in Paris, then Saxony. A huge encyclopedia in 19 sections, number 17 being on plants and trees and their herbal properties.

Printed Herbals

1491 *Hortus Sanitatis* – compiled by publisher Jacob Meydenbach of Mainz. The last of the medieval works on herbs.

1500 *Liber de Arte Distillandi de Simplicibus* – by Hieronymous Braunschweig. The first major work on the techniques of distillation "of the waters of all manner of herbes". (English translation by L. Andrewes 1527.)

1525 *Banckes's Herbal* – anonymous, a quarto volume published by Richard Banckes. Earliest English printed herbal, based on earlier manuscript herbals.

1530 *Herbarum Vivae Eicones* – by Otto Brunfels, a former monk, Lutheran preacher, botanist and also physician. Published in Strasbourg, with realistic illustrations, it began the movement towards a more scientific mindset.

1539 *Kräuter Buch* – by Hieronymus Bock. Rather than repeat Dioscorides, Bock wrote about native plants and was the first to attempt a system of plant classification.

1542 *De Historia Stirpium* – written by Leonhard Fuchs. A scholarly work, which sought to clarify identification of medicinal plants mentioned by Dioscorides, through carefully observed illustrations. Records many new plants introduced to Germany from other parts of the world.

1551–68 *The New Herball* – by William Turner, credited as the "father of English botany". Based on his own observations of native plants but using many of the woodcuts from Fuchs' work.

1554 *Cruydeboeck* – by Rembert Dodoens, physician to the Holy Roman Emperor Maximilian II and professor of botany at Leyden University. A work of botanical importance, which borrowed Fuchs' pictures. (Many English editions, *A Niewe Herbal or History of Plants*, by Henry Lyte in 1578.)

1563 *Coloquios dos Simples* – by Garcia de Orta, a Portuguese doctor who spent time in Goa and produced a book on the plants and medicines of India.

Above *Collecting herbs for the Apothecary's preparations, from a Latin manuscript version of the Herbal of Apuleius.*

Above *Frontispiece to* The Herball, *1597, by John Gerard.*

1569 *Dos libros, el uno que trata de todas las cosas que traen de nuestras Indias Occidentales* – by Nicholas Monardes, a Spaniard, who never himself visited America. His book on the plants of the "New World" became better known by the title of the first English edition: *Joyfull Newes Out of the Newe Founde Worlde,* 1577.

1597 *The Herball or Generall Historie of Plantes* – by John Gerard, gardener and botanist. Based on Dodoens' work, it remains one of the most popular, widely quoted from herbals of all time for the grace of its Elizabethan language.

1629 *Paradisi in Sole Paradisus Terrestris*; **1640** *Theatrum Botanicum* – by John Parkinson. The emphasis in the first is on ornamental planting, the second lists 3,800 plants and their medicinal properties.

1652 *The English Physician* – by Nicholas Culpeper, an astrologer, considered a charlatan by the medical establishment of his day. His book is one of the most popular herbals of all time.

1656 *The Art of Simpling*; **1657** *Adam in Eden* – by William Coles. Less popular, but more readable than Culpeper, who Coles thought was "ignorant". Includes much herb lore.

Later Herbals

With the break between botany and medicine, few great medicinal herbals appeared after the 17th century. Those of note included:

1710 *Botanologia, The English Herbal or History of Plants* – by William Salmon.

1838 *Flora Medica* – written by John Lindley, botanist and lecturer to the Society of Apothecaries, who wrote several important horticultural works.

1931 *A Modern Herbal* – by Mrs M. Grieve. Seminal work on herbs of the 20th century.

Stillroom Books

As well as the learned tomes, written by the medical men of their day, there is a long tradition of more homely recipe (usually spelled "receipt") books, which include instructions on the culinary and cosmetic uses of herbs as well as medicinal remedies. They are sometimes known as "stillroom books". Throughout the 17th and 18th centuries all the big country houses had their own stillroom and women were supposed to be fully conversant in the art of making herbal and culinary preparations.

1585 *The Good Housewife's Jewel and Rare Conceits in Cookery* – by T. Dawson. A comprehensive, informative compilation of herbal recipes.

1594 *Delights for Ladies* – by Sir Hugh Platt. A book to fit in the palm of the hand, subtitled "to adorne their Persons, Tables, Closets & Distillatories with Beauties, Banquets, Perfumes & Waters".

1654 *The Art of Cookery* – by Joseph Cooper, recipes of Charles I's head chef.

1655 *The Queen's Closet Opened* – by W. M. (cook to Queen Henrietta Maria). Includes perfumed, culinary and medicinal preparations.

1668 *Choice and Experimental Receipts* – by Sir Kenelm Digby, Stuart diplomat, with a side interest in cookery, alchemy and herbalism. **1669** *The Closet of Sir Kenelm Digby Opened*. Many medicinal and fragrance recipes.

1719 *Acetaria* – written by John Evelyn. Cookery book by the prolific author and diarist, with a large section on the virtues of salad herbs, picked from the garden.

1719 *The Accomplished Lady's Delight* – by Mrs Mary Eales (confectioner to Queen Anne). Includes recipes for candying many flowers and fruits as well as for perfumes and scented waters.

1723 *The Receipt Book of John Nott* – competent, often workable recipes of the cook to the Duke of Bolton.

1732 *Country Housewife and Ladies Directory* – by R. Bradley. Intriguing cookery recipes.

1775 *The Toilet of Flora* – Anonymous. The title page states: "The Chief Intention of this performance is to point out, and explain to the Fair-Sex, the Methods by which they may preserve and add to their charms." But it is also for "Domestic Economy" and gives methods of preparing herbal baths, essences, pomatums, powders, perfumes, sweet-scented waters and opiates for preserving and whitening teeth.

1784 *The Art of Cooking* – by Mrs Glasse.

1845 *Miss Leslie's Directions for Cookery* – by Eliza Leslie (published USA). Primarily culinary recipes, but also contains directions for making oil of flowers, sweet jars, perfumes and scented bags.

Above *A medieval garden from* Rustican de Cultivement des Terres, *also known as* Les Livres des Prouffits. *British Library.*

Herb Garden Design

A look at traditional herb gardens and their influence on styles for today, followed by how to choose a design and whether to go for a formal or informal approach. Practical projects include step-by-step instructions on making a knot garden, raised bed and herb wheel. There are examples of themed gardens for inspiration, with detailed plans.

Above *A herb garden bounded by trees and a hedge creates an air of mystery.*

Left *Clipped box hedges, geometric lines and topiary recreate 17th-century formality in this design.*

Traditional Herb Gardens

Herbs have been grown in gardens since ancient times, as evidenced in Egyptian frescoes and descriptions of the Roman *Hortus*. However, it is really the monastery gardens of the early Christian era, following the fall of Rome, which begin the Western tradition of the herb garden.

A plan of the Benedictine monastery of St Gall in Switzerland, dating from AD 812, provided a blueprint of the style of garden attached to religious houses and which became central to their life and ministry. There were three distinct areas in this early plan. A physic garden of medicinal plants, which included sage, rosemary, rue and roses, was close to the infirmary. On the other side of this building was the vegetable garden, divided into 18 plots, each designated a single species of plant, many of which we would call herbs. There were cabbages, lettuce, onions, celery, coriander, dill, poppy, radish, garlic, parsley, chervil and fennel. The orchard adjoined, with a large, cross-shaped path at the centre, and included burial plots. At the centre of the enclosed cloister garden was an

Above *Reconstruction of a Tudor garden, with a central "knot", at Southampton, England.*

area of lilies, roses and scented flowers for decorating the church, often known as a "paradise garden".

Monastery gardens were by their nature enclosed. This was a feature, too, of privy gardens belonging to a palace or castle in the medieval period. However, the emphasis here was on enjoyment, with scents, seats and arbours.

Another characteristic of the monastic gardens, which was carried into the designs of the Renaissance period beginning in the 16th century, is the rectangular layout of symmetrical paths, with the cross as a central motif. It has often been noted, however, that the Islamic and Persian tradition of a garden on a grid pattern (probably set out this way for ease of watering by irrigation channels) was also an influence.

In England the fashion for knot gardens began at the outset of the reign of Henry VIII, in the early 16th century, and was popular for over 200 years. Some of the patterns, depicting interlaced ribbons, were extremely complicated and set out in clipped hedges of wall germander, hyssop, cotton lavender and box, infilled with coloured stones or scented herbs and

flowers. By the 17th century the more expansive and open French parterre, with its elaborate swirls of curls and loops, became fashionable.

It was during the 17th century that a host of new plants arrived in Europe, brought back by explorers and traders. Many of the new arrivals were from North America, including nasturtiums and sunflowers. They were planted in physic gardens and the gardens of the great houses, as well as in large botanical gardens throughout Europe, where the study of botany and medicine still went hand in hand. It was a two-way traffic as plants from the "old world" were also taken to North America.

The landscape movement and "natural" school of garden design in the 18th century swept away the intricate knots and parterres; and physic gardens declined in importance as medicine moved apart from botany. Herbs were still grown, of course, but retreated to the cottage garden. Here, they largely remained until the early 20th century when Vita Sackville-West and Gertrude Jekyll started the fashion for informal planting of old-fashioned species, and restored herbs to centre stage.

Above *An elaborate 17th-century garden, from a painting by Johan Walter, 1660.*

Herb Gardens for Today

When planning a herb garden today there is a vast choice of styles and influences to choose from. As herbs and plants cover such a wide range, they are often grown throughout the garden in ornamental beds and borders or among vegetable plots. But a designated herb garden with a range of medicinal, culinary and aromatic plants and its own boundaries always makes a rewarding feature. In a very small garden, of course, it may well be designed to take up the whole area.

Historical precedents provide much inspiration for a herb garden in the formal style, with rectangular beds, straight paths and edgings of clipped box. It could be based on the medieval garden, with narrow, raised beds filled with a single species, divided by wide alleys. Or you could draw inspiration from the romantic enclave of a castle garden; or a cloister or paradise garden. And the striking pattern of a knot garden or parterre is always effective.

Informal designs based on curves and irregular shapes give scope for imaginative planting schemes with a

Above *A beautiful, scented cloister garden at Château de Vandrimare in France.*

bold use of colour and texture; and the cottage-garden style, with its profusion of plants crammed into a small space, is another option.

In any scheme a place to sit, either a simple bench or intricate covered arbour, is a must. A sundial or urn as a centrepiece provides a good focal point.

Whatever the style, some kind of enclosure adds an extra dimension, setting the herb garden apart. It could be a low fence or herbal hedge or, for a larger area, high trelliswork or a wall may be more appropriate. Herbs may be practical plants, for particular purposes, but they also add a little mystery and magic to the world and deserve a special place of their own.

Left *A sundial makes a traditional focal point in an informal planting of herbs and roses, with a statue in the background.*

Choosing a Design

Working out the design of a new herb garden is an exciting project. But before you begin there are several questions you need to answer to ensure that the end result is a success. Space is the first consideration. How much room are you prepared to devote to herbs? Do you have a large enough area to make a garden within a garden? Perhaps you would like to turn most, or all, of your existing space over to herbs? Or would a bed or border of herbs be more appropriate?

Plan how the design is going to fit in with your surroundings. Think about your house and current garden, as this will dictate the overall style you choose; formal, informal, old-fashioned or state-of-the-art or of the 21st century.

Consider how much time and energy you have for upkeep. Beware of choosing a large and complicated scheme if from a practical point of view your needs are for a low-maintenance garden. A simple knot of box hedging, filled in with gravel needs clipping only twice a year. But be wary of putting in other traditional clipped herbs, such as santolina and germander, unless you are prepared to trim the plants frequently. A formal potager, which needs constant replanting and tending to keep it in shape, can be very time-consuming. But a carefully thought-out border of shrubby herbs and perennials needs little upkeep. Containers of herbs can provide extra space and variety.

Consider which category of herbs is your chief interest – culinary, medicinal or scented and aromatic? Your preference here may dictate size, layout and planting plans. If your main aim is to produce a good supply of culinary herbs, a small, formal patch may be sufficient. But if your ambition is to include as many species as possible, a more extensive scheme is inevitable.

Left *A foliage archway and large containers of pelargoniums mark the entrance to an inviting garden bounded by a high hedge.*

Below *Topiary and architectural plants of contrasting foliage lend height and interest to a mixed scheme of herbs.*

Formal Gardens

Taking their inspiration from the Renaissance gardens of France and Italy, formal designs depend on straight lines and geometric shapes, on symmetry and regularity. Balance is the key, with elements arranged around a central axis. The strict pattern of paths, which form the structure, is all-important. Paths may be of brick, stone, gravel or grass, but make sure they are wide enough to walk on comfortably and to take a wheelbarrow. A metre (about three feet) is a minimum width for straight sections, with some wider areas to create a feeling of spaciousness and for extra manoeuvrability. Planting schemes echo the geometry of the layout, with corresponding blocks of colour filling the beds. Foliage plants, especially those with a dense habit of growth such as thyme, are often more suitable than those with a profusion of flowers and a tendency to sprawl.

Large pots and ornaments or statues provide focal points at the ends of vistas. If placed to line a path edge or in a regular pattern they will provide visual links, drawing the scheme together and reinforcing the regularity. Topiary and plants growing over a shaped framework are used in much the same way. They also introduce a theatrical element which underlines the style. But beware of cramming in too much – for this look to be successful, understatement and simplicity are best.

Above *The low-growing silver thyme in the foreground forms a block of colour to reinforce the geometry of the design.*

This plan is for a garden about 11 x 9.50 m (36 x 31 ft), enclosed by a brick wall to one side and trelliswork at each corner supporting a scented, white-flowered jasmine. If you do not have a site where a wall can be used as one boundary, the trellis can be extended. An archway, clothed in the coppery pink climbing rose, 'Albertine', forms the main entrance, with a bench seat under a jasmine arbour on the opposite side, against the wall. Topiary in pots – box trees clipped in spheres and rosemary globes – mark the points of entry, add height to the scheme and increase the sense of regularity.

A sundial surrounded by a chamomile lawn, of the non-flowering cultivar *Chamaemelum nobile* 'Treneague', makes a focal point at the centre, emphasized by the square beds of creeping thymes, bronze-purple 'Russetings' and the white-flowering *Thymus serpyllum* var. 'albus'. Chamomile is quite difficult to establish as a lawn and needs constant weeding, so is best kept on a small scale, as it is here. Paths are of stone slabs with brick or tiling edges to the beds.

The emphasis of the planting is on scented herbs with a purple, silver and white colour scheme predominating. Dark-green hyssop, which has blue flower spikes in summer, along with feathery bronze fennel, provide contrast and texture. Golden hops, trained against the wall, echoed by golden sage, lend brightness. Each of the main beds is edged with a low-growing lavender and has a standard rose at the centre.

Plan for a formal herb garden

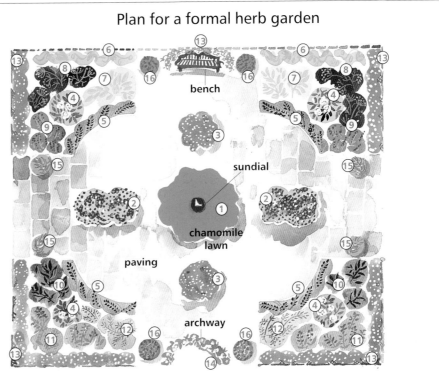

Key to planting plan

1. *Chamaemelum nobile* 'Treneague' – non-flowering chamomile
2. *Thymus serpyllum* 'Russetings' – creeping thyme (mauve-flowering)
3. *Thymus serpyllum* var. 'albus' – creeping thyme (white-flowering)
4. *Rosa* 'Félicité Perpétue' – as a weeping standard
5. *Lavandula angustifolia* 'Hidcote' – low-growing lavender
6. *Humulus lupulus* 'Aureus' – golden hops
7. *Salvia officinalis* 'Icterina' – golden sage
8. *Foeniculum vulgare* 'Purpureum' – bronze fennel
9. *Hyssopus officinalis* – hyssop
10. *Salvia officinalis* Purpura-scens Group – purple sage
11. *Salvia sclarea* – clary sage
12. *Artemisia absinthum* – wormwood
13. *Jasminum officinale* – jasmine
14. *Rosa* 'Albertine' – rose 'Albertine'
15. *Rosmarinus officinalis* – rosemary trained over a globe frame
16. *Buxus sempervirens* – box trained as a "lollipop"

Formal Beds and Borders

Beds edged with low hedges of clipped, dwarf box are a sure way of providing a formal, structured look. This works well for several beds, each being one element of a larger, overall design, or for a single herb border to stand alone.

A large border may also be subdivided by a pattern of internal hedges for a more interesting effect. The spaces in between construct individual planting areas for different species of herb. Timber or tiling edges are another way to give beds a neat finish in a formal scheme.

Right *Tightly clipped box hedging provides an orderly framework for herbs.*

Left *Various designs for long, rectangular borders which are sub-divided by low, internal hedges. Diamonds and squares create satisfying patterns as border divisions and can be filled with a variety of other herbs.*

Above *Pyramids of box and tiling edges give beds a neat finish in a formal scheme.*

Clipped Mounds

Clipped mounds of plants such as cotton lavender, or golden or variegated dwarf box, may be used to great effect, either as edgings or to infill a whole bed. This kind of scheme has more impact if punctuated by clipped plants of a contrasting shape and colour: such as a large bed filled with mounds of silvery santolina, set against pyramids of dark-green box bordering a path.

A formal effect can also be achieved by planting blocks of herbs to make up a simple pattern of squares or triangular shapes, which can be repeated. This works most successfully for herbs of contrasting foliage colour and similar heights and habits: silver posie thyme, perhaps, with the dark green of wall germander, or golden and purple sage.

Topiary Herbs

Standard "mop-head" box or bay trees, pyramids or spiral shapes are an instant way to add formality. If you have time and patience you can train your own to shape, but it may be easier to buy them ready-grown. Topiary and citrus fruit trees in tubs were a popular feature in Tudor and Renaissance gardens, and can still work well in a modern scheme. Placed at strategic points in a geometric scheme, they add an old-fashioned touch and increase the sense of order and regularity. They can also be very useful for introducing the all-important dimension of height and visually linking the various elements of a garden.

Effective herbs for potted topiary include: bay, wall germander, mintbush (*Prostanthera rotundifolia*), rosemary, scented-leaf pelargoniums – especially *P. crispum* – myrtle and box.

Right *A bay tree clipped into a spiral emerges from a sea of lavender.*

Below *Box hedging punctuated by finials, tall clipped shapes in the beds and the trim, rounded heads of an avenue of* Quercus ilex *add up to topiary on a grand scale.*

Knot Gardens

Pattern is very satisfying to the eye and a knot garden always makes a stunning feature. The historic ideal consisted of four elements, each of a different pattern, but it would be as well to start with something simpler.

An area 3–4 m (10–13 ft) square will be large enough to contain an interesting, interwoven pattern. If possible it should be sited where it can be viewed from above – an upstairs window, neighbouring mound or raised level in the garden. It could also form an attractive centrepiece of a sunken garden. A sunny position and well-drained soil will suit it best. The old pattern books include a wide variety of hedging plants for knot gardens. To do the job effectively the

plants need to be evergreens with small leaves, dense growth and an ability to withstand close clipping. Although they all have attractive flowers and are not as neat and compact as box, excellent results can be obtained with the following herbs:

Teucrium chamaedrys has glossy, dark-green foliage, shaped like oak leaves. It is fully hardy and tolerates hard trimming, and is easy to grow from cuttings. Plant 23 cm (9 in) apart.

Santolina chamaecyparissus has silvery foliage. This responds well to close clipping and regenerates from old wood. Plant cuttings approximately 23 cm (9 in) apart. *Santolina rosmarinifolia* and *Santolina viridis* have acid-green leaves, treat these as *S. chamaecyparissus*.

Hyssopus officinalis has dark green foliage and is semi-evergreen. This often loses its leaves where winters are hard, but regenerates from old wood. Clip it regularly to avoid straggling and replace plants every four or five years. Plant 23 cm (9 in) apart.

Lavandula angustifolia 'Hidcote' – A low-growing lavender with silvery foliage. Immediately after flowering clip back to shape. However, do not cut into any old wood.

Using box for knot gardens

Box is ideal for knot gardens as its neat habit of growth means that it retains a clipped shape better than most plants. However, it is relatively slow-growing, and an instant finished effect is not easy to achieve.

Buxus sempervirens 'Suffruticosa' has bright-green leaves and is a compact plant, ideal for all edging work.

Buxus sempervirens 'Elegantissima' with small, silver-edged, olive-green leaves is slow-growing and makes a good contrast for darker leaves. *Buxus microphylla* 'Koreana' is low-growing and has dense, dark-green leaves.

It is best to choose compact varieties of box such as these, or the garden will soon grow unwieldy. Using all box makes a more manageable scheme than interspersing other knot garden plants, with different rates of growth and heights when mature.

'Elegantissima'   'Suffruticosa'   'Koreana'

Above *This striking pattern in the form of a foot maze at Hatfield House, England, symbolizes the complexities of following the Christian path through life.*

Right *A stunning and colourful knot garden of clipped box, with spaces between hedges filled with roses, lavender and scented herbs.*

To make a simple knot garden

Tips for success:

• Prepare the site well. Dig in some garden compost or manure, as it will be difficult to add organic matter once the plants are established.

• Make sure the area is completely level – use boards and a carpenter's spirit level.

• Accuracy of measuring out the design and putting in the plants is essential. A large set square, made of lengths of wood nailed together in the proportion of 3:4:5, ensures accurate 90° angles at the corners.

1 Draw the plan out on graph paper in measurements to suit your plot (3–4 m or 10–13 sq ft). Colour in the design to represent the plants to be used to achieve the effect of interwoven ribbons.

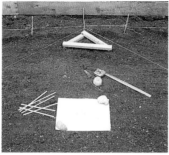

2 Using the plan as a guide, mark out the squares on the ground using the tape measure, string and short lengths of cane. A builder's square will ensure accurate right angles.

3 Find the centre point of each side of the outer square and mark the semi-circles by drawing arcs with string attached to a cane. The string should be the length of the radius of the semi-circles.

4 Mark out the semi-circle with the pointed canes and attach the string tautly to define the curve. This provides an accurate guide to follow when delineating the design in sand.

5 Mark out the rest of the design with string and canes, measuring everything carefully. To define the pattern, fill a plastic bottle with fine sand and pour it out evenly along the lines of the string and all markings. Remove the string and canes.

6 Put in the plants, spacing them evenly, 15 cm (6 in) apart and keeping accurately to the markings. Follow the colour code on the plan, making sure the interwoven effect is achieved by putting the right colour plant at the intersections.

7 It will take two to three years for the plants to develop and close the gaps. In the second year, pinch out the centres and trim lightly to encourage growth. Once filled out, clip twice a year (late spring and early autumn). Avoid clipping if there is any danger of frost, as the new soft growth will be damaged by it.

Informal Gardens

Designs based on fluid shapes and an irregular layout give plenty of scope for growing a variety of herbs. They often fit better than formal schemes with the style of a contemporary house and surroundings. Paths may be offset and gently curving, with beds and borders placed seemingly at random. Areas of hard material are often broken by greenery and flowers. Plants spill over on to the paths and spring up among the pea shingle; gaps are left among the paving stones of a terrace to be filled with creeping, aromatic herbs. Bare expanses of plant-free gravel are not in keeping with this style of garden.

Planting should be exuberant: forests of poppies, stands of valerian, a vibrant jumble of flowers and foliage. Pruning and trimming are, of course, essential, but the close-clipped look is less acceptable here.

This is not to say that the structure of the informal garden has to be completely irregular. A relaxed look is frequently achieved by the planting schemes as much as by the layout of beds and paths. This has its roots in the cottage garden genre of gardening, where a central path divided two rectangular areas, and lack of space forced an eclectic mix of plants.

In many informal gardens a regular framework works well. But it has to be simple – four rectangular beds, divided by intersecting paths, perhaps. There is little room for complex patterns and rigid symmetry.

Above *Exuberant planting in a cottage garden style.*

Above *Irregular circular shapes and a gently winding path in a display garden at the National Herb Centre, England.*

Plan for an informal herb garden

This has been designed as a peaceful, rustic retreat as well as being an all-purpose herb garden containing a wide variety of plants. A path of circular logs, laid at the side of the central sweep of gravel, leads around the edge of a pond to a wooden decking area for seating and a table. Creeping thymes are planted in pockets among the log paving, and architectural spires of mullein, *Verbascum thapsus*, spring up at random in the gravel.

The borders at either side are planted for colour and to provide a selection of culinary herbs as well. A further collection of culinary herbs in containers is sited near the seating area, and an olive tree in a tub (so that it can be moved to a protected area for winter) is near the entrance. This is surrounded by shrubby herbs: thyme, sage, prostrate rosemary and winter savory in a gravel mulch, which echoes the main area of gravel.

For early summer colour there are swathes of red and white valerian and opium poppies, to be followed later in the season by brilliant red bergamot, *Monarda didyma* 'Cambridge Scarlet'. A broad band of blue catmint, *Nepeta* x *faassenii*, leads the eye up to the pond, where the fine mossy growth of Corsican mint, *Mentha requienii*, spills over the logs, with clumps of chives and gold and green variegated gingermint nearby. An ornamental form of sweet flag, *Acorus gramineus* 'Variegatus', which does not grow as large as the more authentic sweet flag, *Acorus calamus*, is planted in the pond with some water lilies.

Behind the pond, the spearmint is planted in a bucket with no base to prevent it spreading. Angelica, lovage and fennel provide height and texture as well as being valuable culinary herbs. At the top of the garden, just on its boundaries, is a common elder, with golden and fern-leafed varieties for extra interest.

To complete the countryside feel of the garden and continue the timber theme the boundary could be further defined by traditional wicker screening.

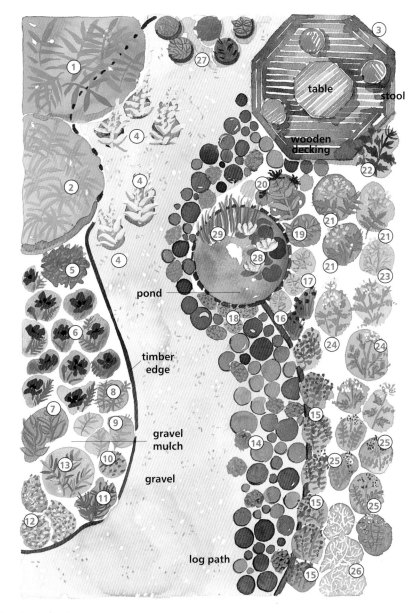

Key to planting plan

1. *Sambucus nigra* – common elder
2. *Sambucus nigra* 'Aurea' – golden elder
3. *Sambucus nigra* f. *laciniata* – fern-leafed elder
4. *Verbascum thapsus* – mullein
5. *Origanum onites* – pot marjoram
6. *Papaver somniferum* – opium poppy has white or lilac flowers, but there are many attractive cultivars in reds and pinks
7. *Salvia officinalis* – common sage
8. *Artemisia dracunculus* – tarragon
9. *Satureja montana* – winter savory

10. *Thymus vulgaris* – common thyme
11. *Rosmarinus officinalis* – prostratus group – prostrate rosemary
12. *Thymus vulgaris* 'Silver Posie' – silver posie thyme
13. *Olea europaea* – olive tree
14. *Thymus serpyllum* 'Bressingham Pink' – creeping thymes and *T. serpyllum* Coccineus
15. *Nepeta* x *faassenii* – catmint
16. *Allium schoenoprasum* – chives
17. *Mentha* x *gracilis* 'Variegata' – gingermint
18. *Mentha requienii* – Corsican mint
19. *Mentha spicata* – spearmint

20. *Monarda didyma* 'Cambridge-Scarlet' – bergamot, red flowering
21. *Angelica archangelica* – angelica
22. *Levisticum officinale* – lovage
23. *Foeniculum vulgare* – fennel
24. *Valeriana officinalis* – white valerian
25. *Centranthus ruber* – red valerian
26. *Helichrysum italicum* – curry plant
27. A selection of culinary herbs in pots
28. *Nymphaea odorata* – white water lily
29. *Acorus gramineus* 'Variegatus' – variegated sweet flag

Herbal Beds and Borders

Island beds or long borders can make gratifying small herb gardens where space is limited. They are ideal for providing a supply of herbs for cooking, or a colourful medley of medicinal and aromatic herbs for general household use. In larger beds, paths or narrow brick divisions may be appropriate as visual separations and to prevent invasive species from growing into each other. Stepping stones, placed in a random pattern, provide easy access to the plants for picking or weeding.

When planting island beds, tall subjects, such as angelica and lovage, may be placed at the centre, with lower growing plants surrounding them. In a border against a wall or hedge, plant heights look best graduated, with the tallest at the back and dwarf and creeping plants at the front. Introducing height with statuesque plants adds interest. Standards, especially of plants with irregular growth patterns – olive trees, lemon verbena, old-fashioned roses – also add extra height. Scented climbing plants, such as jasmine, hops or honeysuckle, trained over tepees of canes or wooden sticks, make unusual punctuation marks in a large border.

Above *A simple, rectangular border with paved divisions, set in a gravel surround, makes a self-contained herb garden.*

Left *Bronze fennel contrasts well with white-flowering* Galega officinalis *'Alba'.*

Below *A river of creeping thymes, flanked at right by gallica roses (*R. g. var. officinalis *and* R. g. *'Versicolor'), makes an imaginative and decorative feature.*

Above *Closely packed herbs provide a riot of midsummer colour.*

Right *Alternating clumps of purple and green-leafed sage,* Salvia officinalis.

Below *A pocket of mixed thymes, set in golden stone.*

Raised Beds

These have many advantages. They can be used to provide ideal conditions where garden soil is unsuitable. If your garden is on heavy clay, which most herbs dislike, especially the shrubby, Mediterranean varieties, a raised bed can offer the requisite free-draining environment. Where soil is poor and dry, a raised bed can be filled with a good moisture-retentive growing medium for herbs that need damp ground. Beds at a higher level can also make gardening easier and more rewarding for the disabled or elderly. For everyone, they allow plants to be seen from a new perspective so that flowers, foliage and scents can all be appreciated more closely.

Heights of raised beds may be varied according to intended purpose or preference. Old illustrations reveal the popularity from medieval times into the age of the Renaissance garden, of beds raised from the surrounding paths by no more than a few inches. For old-style physic gardens and formal potagers, low raised beds, edged with timber, are both practical and decorative.

Above *A brick-built raised bed provides a free-draining environment, which suits many herbs, especially those of Mediterranean origin.*

There are various materials that can be used for constructing raised beds:

Timber – use planks that are wide enough to sink into the ground. Screw or nail together securely at the corners and treat with wood preservative suitable for plants.

Railway sleepers (railroad ties) can be used for a rustic, informal look. Clean off any tar and preservatives, which are toxic to plants, with solvent. A plastic membrane may be necessary for heavily impregnated sleepers. No foundations are necessary as their weight makes them stable. Lay them flat, rather than on edge, for stability and fix together at the corners with steel rods, driven through them and into the ground.

Bricks are durable and attractive in a variety of settings (especially old bricks). Check they are frostproof as ordinary housebricks may not be suitable.

Above *A raised bed made of timber with feverfew and grasses.*

Above *Marjorams growing in a bed walled with stone.*

Above *Herbs flourish in a brick-built raised bed.*

Making a raised bed

Raised beds can be laid out as functional squares and rectangles, in decorative shapes or made to fit a corner of the garden such as this bed for culinary herbs.

YOU WILL NEED

Short stakes or dowel; string; builder's set square; fine sand or line-marker paint; tape measure; cement; ballast; builder's sand; pointing trowel; approximately 90 bricks; spirit level; waterproof paint; paintbrush; rubble; gravel or pea shingle (pea stone); 3 bags of topsoil; potting medium; a selection of herbs

1 *Mark out the shape of the bed on the ground, using a short, pointed stake or dowel and string. Use a builder's set square to ensure correct right angles. Define the lines with a dribble of fine sand, or use line-marker paint.*

2 *Dig out the soil along the markings to a depth and width of 15 cm (6 in). Fill in with concrete to within 5 cm (2 in) of the top. Firm down, level and leave for 24 hours to set completely. For concrete, use one part cement to four parts ballast.*

3 *Build up four or five courses of bricks, and set into mortar, carefully checking with a spirit level at each stage. (Mortar is one part cement to four parts sharp or builder's sand.)*

4 *Clean up the mortar, while it is still wet, with a pointing trowel. Leave it to harden.*

5 *Before filling with soil, coat the inside of the wall with a waterproof paint.*

6 *Put in a layer of rubble, topped with gravel or pea shingle for drainage. Fill in with bought topsoil and stir in a top layer of a good potting medium.*

7 *Plant up the raised bed with your chosen herbs.*

8 *The completed raised bed planted with a selection of culinary herbs and wild strawberries.*

Herb Wheels

These were a feature of numerous Victorian gardens, when old cartwheels (wagon wheels) were plentiful. They provided frameworks of little beds containing kitchen herbs, the spokes prevented the different varieties from encroaching on each other. If you are using an old cartwheel, it must be treated with a plant-friendly preservative to prevent the timber from rotting. The spokes may also be a little close together to be practical, so consider removing some of them.

A brick-built wheel is long-lasting and the sections can be more effectively allocated. Choose a location in full sun if possible, and if it is for culinary herbs, put it near the kitchen.

Above *An intriguing design for a herb wheel at the Henry Doubleday Research Association.*

Above *Nasturtiums are good in salads.*

Above *Pot marigolds add bright colour to a herb garden.*

Above *Chives and golden marjoram.*

Herbs for a cook's herb wheel

Medium- to low-growing herbs of similar heights make for a balanced effect.

Perennial selection:

Allium schoenoprasum – Chives. Mild onion flavour herb with attractive, purple flowers.

Origanum onites – Pot marjoram. Warm-flavoured leaves, with pinkish-purple flowers.

Satureja montana – Winter savory. Makes an aromatic, neat pillow of dark-green foliage with white flowers.

Thymus x *citriodorus* – Thyme. Delicious, lemon-scented thyme.

Salvia officinalis Purpurascens Group – Purple sage. Bold purple and green foliage; strong, savoury taste.

Foeniculum vulgare – Fennel. Tall, feathery plant with an aniseed flavour for central pot.

Petroselinum crispum – Parsley. Biennial. It is also suitable for growing as an annual.

Annual selection to sow from seed:

Calendula officinalis – Pot marigold. Well worth including for the brilliance of its flowers. Self-seeds.

Anthriscus cerefolium – Chervil. A delicately flavoured herb, which is fully hardy and can be sown successionally for a continuous supply. Self-seeds.

Coriandrum sativum – Coriander (Cilantro). Spicy flavour. Thin out seedlings and keep moist.

Tropaeolum majus – Nasturtium. Grow it for the bright flowers and use them in salads.

Ocimum basilicum 'Purple Ruffles' – Purple basil. The foliage provides a foil for other green herbs. Good basil flavour.

Satureja hortensis – Summer savory. This is more subtly flavoured than the perennial variety and it goes very well with beans.

Anethum graveolens – Dill. Plant in the central pot for its feathery foliage and delicate taste.

Making a raised brick herb wheel

1 *Using a length of string equal to the radius of the bed, attached to a piece of pointed cane, mark out a circle on the ground. Then shorten the string and mark a small inner circle at the centre. Sink a length of earthenware (clay) sewage pipe (from builder's merchants or building supply stores) in the centre. Then measure off equal points on the circumference to form the spokes, marking them out with canes and string.*

2 *Trace over the whole design with fine sand or line-marker paint.*

3 *Dig a trench for the bricks and fill with sharp or builder's sand.*

4 *Construct as for the raised bed (steps 3–5), putting in one or two layers of bricks, set in mortar, to form the outer circle and spokes.*

5 *Fill in the sections of the wheel and the earthenware pipe with rubble, then gravel or pea shingle, topsoil and compost (soil mix).*

YOU WILL NEED

String; short canes or dowel; earthenware (clay) sewage pipe; fine sand or line-marker paint; tape measure; sharp sand; approximately 90 bricks; cement; builder's sand; ballast; pointing trowel; spirit level; waterproof paint; rubble; gravel or pea shingle; 3 bags of topsoil; compost (soil mix); a selection of culinary herbs

6 *Plant the herb wheel with a selection of culinary herbs such as wild strawberry, thyme, sage, rosemary and lemon verbena.*

Themed Gardens

A themed garden can make a vibrant and colourful display for herbs. In the following section there are plans for various styles of gardens – an old-fashioned medieval garden, a decorative Shakespearean garden with a small knot garden of clipped box, and a pot-pourri garden with many different fragrant herbs and scented flowers. The cook's or kitchen garden is not only productive but will look good too.

The potager is intended mainly for culinary use but with bold use of colour, it makes an excellent ornamental layout. The plan for a traditional apothecary's garden with small, individual plots of medicinal herbs shows how to make a functional, but very eye-catching, herb garden, that needs the bare minimum of maintenance.

Right *A re-creation of a medieval pleasure garden with scented herbs, at Tretower Court, Wales.*

Medieval Garden

Above *Herbs such as valerian and feverfew grow in the raised beds of this medieval-style garden. When gardens like this were laid out, beauty was not a consideration, but with their symmetry, and the colours and shapes of the plants, the effect is delightful.*

In gardens of the Middle Ages herbs were often grown in small beds, each devoted to a single species. This made it easy to tend and harvest the plants, as well as to identify them, and was the chosen style of monastery and physic gardens, whose primary purpose was practical.

By the 12th and 13th centuries pleasure gardens, based on cloister gardens, became a feature of palaces and castles. These usually took the form of a small enclosed "privy" garden, for the benefit of the lady of the house and her attendants. King Henry III installed one for his queen, stipulating that it should have a pleasant herbery and high walls so that no one should enter except the Queen. There are narrow beds at the side, and a seat or an arbour is standard, and often there is a fountain splashing in the corner.

Plan for a medieval garden

This small garden, designed to take up approximately 6 x 8 m (19 x 26 ft), is surrounded by a trellis, with a low fence on one side and a Gothic arch as entranceway. Since a "flowery mead" would be an impractical proposition in this space, the path is made of gravel, with a central bed of pot marigolds, surrounded by a chamomile lawn.

Two chamomile seats, made as raised beds, are separated by a gallica rose, with further gallica roses at opposite corners.

Rosa eglanteria, the eglantine rose of Chaucer's day, climbs over the trellis, but a compromise has been made with the other climbing rose, 'Noisette Carnée'. This rose, unlike the others, is not ancient enough to be a true medieval rose, but has a delicate old-fashioned form and the great benefit of repeat flowering to provide interest over a longer period.

Narrow beds against the perimeter are planted with a froth of lady's mantle, flax (with its profusion of dainty blue flowers),

feverfew, wild strawberries and other plants common at the time – though a modern cultivar, *Achillea millefolium* 'Moonshine', has been substituted for wild yarrow, which would be too invasive for the area and not very attractive. There is a small fountain and shallow pond in one corner, with the moisture-loving *Iris versicolor* planted at its margins. White Madonna lilies, popular in the medieval era as a symbol of purity and associated with the Virgin Mary, are planted in pots.

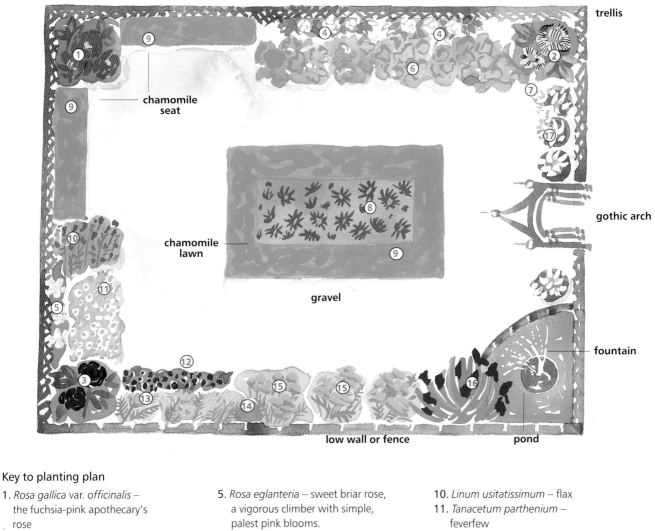

trellis

chamomile seat

chamomile lawn

gravel

gothic arch

fountain

pond

low wall or fence

Key to planting plan

1. *Rosa gallica* var. *officinalis* – the fuchsia-pink apothecary's rose
2. *Rosa gallica* var. *officinalis* 'Versicolor' – pink-and-white-striped gallica rose
3. *Rosa gallica* var. *officinalis* 'Tuscany Superb' – dark-crimson, double gallica
4. *Rosa* 'Noisette Carnée' (syn. 'Blush Noisette') – pale-pink repeat-flowering climber
5. *Rosa eglanteria* – sweet briar rose, a vigorous climber with simple, palest pink blooms.
6. *Alchemilla mollis* – lady's mantle
7. *Thymus vulgaris* 'Silver Posie' – thyme with silver-variegated foliage
8. *Calendula officinalis* – pot marigold
9. *Chamaemelum nobile* 'Treneague' – a non-flowering chamomile
10. *Linum usitatissimum* – flax
11. *Tanacetum parthenium* – feverfew
12. *Fragaria vesca* – wild strawberry
13. *Tanacetum vulgare* – tansy
14. *Thymus vulgaris* – thyme
15. *Achillea millefolium* 'Moonshine'
16. *Iris versicolor* – blue flag
17. *Lilium candidum* – Madonna lily

Shakespearean Garden

For those with a literary bent, a garden based on the herbs and flowers included in the works of Shakespeare makes an exciting project. No other poet and playwright can have made so many references to these plants, nor indicated such a delight in them and knowledge of their uses and characteristics. There is also scope for a comprehensive selection, as over 130 plants are mentioned, some under two or three different names.

Culinary herbs include "saffron to colour the warden pies", "a dish of caraways" (caraway seeds) to eat with apples and "parsley to stuff a rabbit". Garlic gets several mentions, usually in connection with its odour on the breath, and onions are linked with tears.

Medicinal uses of plants make frequent entrances – though the portrait of the downtrodden apothecary (in *Romeo and Juliet*) with his "old cakes of roses" and other accoutrements "thinly scattered to make up a show" is hardly a flattering one. The narcotic properties of poppies and mandrake are referred to several times and the myth that mandrakes scream when uprooted is perpetuated. The power of the witch's brew is noted, with its deadly "root of hemlock digged i' the dark". The symbolic associations of herbs are acknowledged such as wormwood for bitterness, and also rosemary for remembrance.

Household uses of herbs include polishing chairs with juice of balm in *The Merry Wives of Windsor*; and the soothing power of scented flowers is memorably evoked in Oberon's description of Titania's bower in *A Midsummer Night's Dream*:

I know a bank whereon the wild thyme blows,
Where oxlips and the nodding violet grows
Quite over-canopied with luscious woodbine [honeysuckle],
With sweet musk-roses, and with eglantine.

Who could resist re-creating this for themselves? For researching the full extent of Shakespeare's references to herbs, *Shakespeare Concordance* by A. Bartlett, 1894, is a great help.

Other works include: *The Plant-lore and Garden Craft of Shakespeare* – by Rev. Henry N. Ellacombe, 1884; *The Flora and Folklore of Shakespeare* – by F.G. Savage (Shakespeare Press, 1923); *The Shakespeare Garden* – by Esther Singleton (William Farquhar Payson, New York, 1931); *Shakespeare's Wild Flowers* – by Eleanour Sinclair Rohde (the Medici Society 1935); *The Flowers of Shakespeare* – by Doris Hunt (Webb and Bower, 1980).

Above *Box and cotton lavender form intertwining ribbons in a garden edging.*

Top *The flower stems of silvery blue* Echevarias *create an intricate pattern.*

Above *Lavender grows very well in the free-draining soil of a bed with raised timber edge.*

Opposite *An Elizabethan knot garden, closely planted with colourful flowers for a richly embroidered effect, at Stratford-upon-Avon, England.*

Plan for a Shakespearean garden

The plan is for a garden approximately 9 x 13 m (29 x 43 ft) in the formal style that was popular in Shakespeare's day. At the centre is a small knot garden of clipped box, surrounded by narrow borders of lavender and pinks. Three spacious steps lead to an arbour on a higher level, so that the knot can be viewed from above. Creeping thyme is planted in pockets on the stone slabs in front of the seat, and over the steps. The arbour is clad in honeysuckle and roses and surrounded by the 'wild thyme' and other flowers and herbs of Titania's bower. Raised beds, with brick-retaining walls, form the boundaries and topiary trees in tubs visually link the garden and mark the entrance points. Poisonous plants such as hemlock, henbane, aconitum and others have not been included in this garden for safety reasons. The two rue bushes are at the back of the border, where they are least likely to be accidentally brushed. Rue can cause blistering on contact, but has long been a popular aromatic plant.

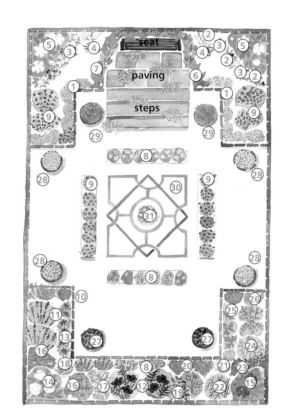

Key to planting plan

1. *Thymus serpyllum* – wild thyme
2. *Viola odorata/Viola tricolor* violets and heartsease
3. *Primula veris/Primula vulgaris* – cowslips/primrose
4. *Lilium candidum* – Madonna lily
5. *Rosa moschata* – musk rose
6. *Rosa eglanteria* – sweet briar rose
7. *Lonicera periclymenum* – honeysuckle
8. *Dianthus caesius/Dianthus deltoides* – pinks
9. *Lavandula angustifolia* 'Hidcote' – lavender

10. *Satureja montana* – winter savory
11. *Consolida ajacis* – larkspur
12. *Papaver somniferum* – opium poppies
13. *Calendula officinalis* – pot marigold
14. *Rosa x alba* – white rose of York
15. *Rosa gallica* var. *officinalis* – red rose of Lancaster
16. *Ruta graveolens* – rue
17. *Artemisia absinthum* – wormwood
18. *Hyssopus officinalis* – hyssop
19. *Origanum onites* – marjoram
20. *Mentha* spp. – mint
21. *Carum carvi* – caraway

22. *Foeniculum vulgare* – fennel
23. *Borago officinalis* – borage
24. *Melissa officinalis* 'Aurea' – variegated lemon balm
25. *Petroselinum crispum* – parsley
26. *Sanguisorba minor* – salad burnet
27. *Laurus nobilis* – standard bay
28. *Buxus sempervirens* – standard box
29. *Rosmarinus officinalis* – rosemary (trained as topiary)
30. *Buxus sempervirens* 'Suffruticosa' – dwarf box
31. *Myrtus communis* subsp. *tarentina* – dwarf myrtle

Pot-pourri Garden

There is a long tradition of drying scented flowers and aromatic herbs for sweetening the air. Stillroom books of the 17th and 18th centuries include many recipes for scented powders and "perfumes" as pot-pourri was more usually known then. The term as currently used to describe a mixture of dried fragrant petals and leaves did not become common until the 19th century. It comes from the name of a Spanish stew, *olla podrida* (literally meaning "rotten pot"), and the French translation of pot-pourri came to mean any medley or mixture.

An area of scented herbs and flowers, which can be picked for pot-pourri, makes a rewarding garden feature. Stock it with plenty of roses – pink and red ones are best as they retain good colour when dried.

"Rose-leaves ... were gathered even as they fell to make into a pot-pourri for someone who had no garden." (*Cranford* by Mrs Gaskell).

Above *A pergola covered in old-fashioned roses provides plenty of petals for drying.*

Plan for a pot-pourri garden

This plan would fit into an area about 8 m (26 ft) square to make a scented garden with plenty of material to cut for making pot-pourri. The four corner beds, set in a grass path, are edged with dwarf box and filled with colourful flowers and fragrant herbs. The central circular area is brick-paved, with pockets for a low-growing double chamomile and vivid caraway thyme. The gazebo supports a richly perfumed, dark crimson 'Ena Harkness' climbing rose and a cloud of jasmine. There is room beneath it for a seat, or a small table and some stools, and it is surrounded by pots of colourful, scented pelargoniums, pineapple sage and lemon verbena.

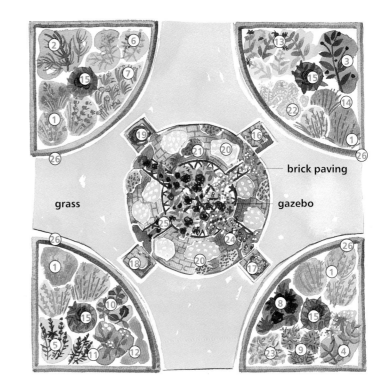

grass

brick paving

gazebo

Key to planting plan

1. *Lavandula angustifolia* 'Munstead' – dark blue, low-growing lavender
2. *Rosmarinus officinalis* – rosemary
3. *Myrtus communis* – myrtle
4. *Angelica archangelica* – angelica
5. *Agastache foeniculum* – anise hyssop
6. *Hyssopus officinalis* – hyssop
7. *Dianthus* 'London Delight' – an old-fashioned pink
8. *Paeonia officinalis* 'Rubra Plena' – a rich red paeony
9. *Artemisia abrotanum* – southernwood
10. *Coriandrum sativum* – coriander (cilantro)
11. *Tanacetum balsamita* – alecost
12. *Consolida ajacis* – larkspur
13. *Monarda* 'Croftway Pink' – a pink bergamot
14. *Iris germanica* var. *florentina* – Orris
15. *Rosa* 'François Juranville' – a gold-pink rose, as a weeping standard
16. *Aloysia triphylla* – lemon verbena
17. *Pelargonium tomentosum* – peppermint scented
18. *Pelargonium* 'Lady Plymouth' – scented-leaf geranium, with cream margins
19. *Salvia elegans* – pineapple sage
20. *Chamaemelum nobile* 'Flore Pleno' – dwarf, double-flowered chamomile
21. *Thymus herba-barona* – caraway-scented thyme
22. *Thymus vulgaris* 'Silver Posie' – a silver-leafed thyme
23. *Mentha* x *gracilis* 'Variegata' – gingermint
24. *Jasminum officinale* – the white-flowering jasmine
25. *Rosa* 'Ena Harkness' – dark-red climbing rose
26. *Buxus sempervirens* 'Suffruticosa' – dwarf box

To make a rose pot-pourri

Making your own pot-pourri is a rewarding and creative experience. The results will have individuality and a more pleasant fragrance than shop-bought.

YOU WILL NEED

3 cups dried rose petals;
2 cups mixed dried flowers;
15 ml (1 tbsp) dried lavender;
1 cup mixed dried herbs: mint, marjoram, thyme and angelica;
5 ml (1 tsp) cloves; 2.5 ml/½ tsp) ground allspice; 10 ml (2 tsp) ground orris root; 5–10 drops rose essential oil

1 To dry the plant material, pick everything on a dry day. Spread out on newspaper and leave in a warm, airy place (out of direct sunlight) for 5–7 days, until papery to the touch.

2 To make the pot-pourri, combine all the ingredients, mix thoroughly and put them in an airtight container. Leave in a dry, warm place for 2–3 weeks, shaking the container occasionally.

Above *A traditional rose garden in full bloom and (right) a garden of scented herbs and flowers for making pot-pourri.*

Cook's Garden

A small border or bed can provide a surprisingly good selection of herbs to meet basic culinary needs, especially if supplemented by a few tubs and containers. A sunny location is important as the herbs will thrive and have a better flavour. For convenience the kitchen garden should be sited as close to the kitchen door as possible so that herbs can be harvested without you having to trudge too far.

Plan for a cook's garden of herbs

A semicircular-shaped bed against a wall allows space for 13 useful herbs, with bay, basil and mint in containers: tender basil is much easier to grow in a pot, and mint is inclined to spread into its neighbours. A narrow brick path divides the space and makes it easier to reach the plants when tending or picking them.

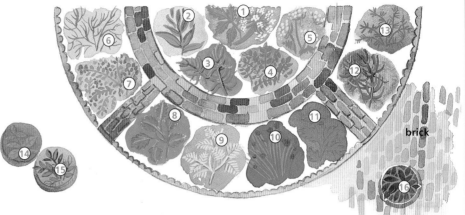

brick path

brick

tubs

Key to planting plan

1. *Angelica archangelica* – angelica
2. *Salvia officinalis* – sage
3. *Artemisia dracunculus* – tarragon
4. *Origanum onites* – pot marjoram
5. *Levisticum officinale* – lovage
6. *Anethum graveolens* – dill
7. *Thymus vulgaris* or *Thymus* x *citriodorus* – thyme or lemon thyme
8. *Coriandrum sativum* – coriander (cilantro)
9. *Anthriscus cerefolium* – chervil
10. *Allium schoenoprasum* – chives
11. *Petroselinum crispum* – parsley
12. *Rosmarinus officinalis* Prostratus Group – prostrate rosemary
13. *Satureja montana* – winter savory
14. *Ocimum basilicum* – sweet basil
15. *Mentha spicata* – spearmint
16. *Laurus nobilis* – bay

Above left *An informal kitchen herb garden with nasturtiums and coriander (cilantro).*

Far left *A pot of golden and purple sage provides a ready source of leaves for cooking.*

Left *Sweet basil is a traditional complementary flavour for tomatoes and is frequently used in culinary dishes.*

Potager

A potager is a garden where vegetables and herbs are grown together in an ornamental layout. Early cooks' gardens contained as many herbs as "vegetables" – as we now call them – with little distinction being made between the two. "Sallet" (salad) herbs in Elizabethan times included a wide variety of unusual leaves and colourful flowers. They were also made into stuffings and uncooked sweet and savoury sauces: flower petals pulverized with ground almonds and sugar, or potent mixtures of green herbs pounded together in vinegar.

Growing herbs and vegetables together is practical and ornamental at the same time. Mixed plantings of this nature suffer less from pests because the bright flowers of many herbs attract beneficial insects, such as lacewings and ladybirds (bugs). At the same time, aromatic plants deter aphids and other insects. If vegetables are intermingled with strong-smelling herbs, rather than planted in huge blocks on their own, they become a less obvious target for the pests normally attracted to them.

As with all vegetable growing, allowance must be made for rotation of crops and there will inevitably be bare patches at intervals to accommodate this. But the garden is afforded a permanent structure by the framework of paths and perennial herbs.

Paths may be of gravel, brick, stone or any hard material. The central one should be at least 1 m (3 ft) wide and the divisions between the beds no less than 0.5 m (20 in). Beds should be no more than 1.5 m (5 ft) wide so that they are easy to reach; timber or tiling edges give them a neat finish and link the elements of the garden together.

Archways for climbing plants at the entrance or at the centre of the garden add height and visual appeal. Espaliered fruit trees at the perimeter make a practical and decorative screen. A tunnelled archway of apples or pears is a traditional feature.

Plan for a potager garden

This potager is both practical and ornamental, with beds about 1.5 m (5 ft) in length and paths 0.5 m (20 in) wide. The plan below allows for perennial herbs, such as lavender, rosemary and sage, to be planted at the ends of each bed.

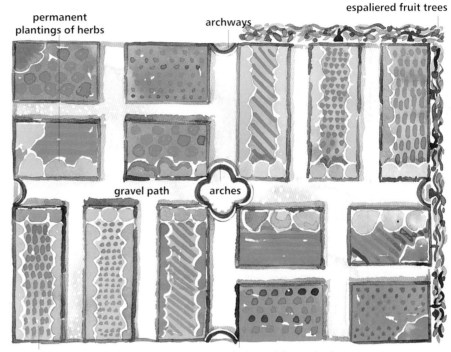

permanent plantings of herbs

archways

espaliered fruit trees

gravel path

arches

vegetables to be grown in rotation

timber edging to beds

Above *A formal potager of box-edged beds, packed with sturdy vegetables, ruby chard (foreground), sweetcorn, marrow and beans, interspersed with aromatic rosemary.*

Apothecary's Garden

Also known as a "physic garden", the apothecary's garden was the source of raw materials for making medicines to heal the sick.

In the tradition of the monasteries, a range of "simples", or medicinal plants, were grown in their own little plots. These were sometimes prescribed to be used on their own, or, more frequently, the apothecary concocted compounds from them, consisting of several ingredients. The advantage of keeping each herb in its separate bed in this way was to make identification easier when it came to picking, as well as being an efficient method of cultivation on a small scale. It also provided easy access for planting, weeding and watering.

When making their remedies, the apothecaries were guided by a variety of herbals: the earliest of which was written in China nearly 5,000 years ago. They also studied the works of the great physicians of ancient Greece – Hippocrates, Galen, Theophrastrus and Dioscorides – and the texts from the Dark Ages which were

copied by generations of monks, and given a new lease of life by the invention of printing in the mid-15th century.

The role and influence of the apothecary began to wane during the 16th century as European herbalists started to base their work on empirical observations of plants. John Gerard's *Herball or Generall Historie of Plantes* was in this tradition of enquiry and was first published in England in 1597. Apothecaries established their own society at the beginning of the 16th century and were the pharmacists of the time, dispensing drugs for the physicians and giving out medical advice to patients.

Above *Herbs growing in little beds, created by gaps in paving slabs, make an attractive and practical medicinal garden.*

Left *A collection of herbs in sunken pots, carefully labelled to ensure correct identification.*

A modern garden of herbs for making home remedies, which draws on the best of these traditions, has understated charm and is a low-maintenance way to grow herbs. Filled with traditional herbs, such as bright gold pot marigolds (*Calendula officinalis*), neatly patterned houseleek (*Sempervivum tectorum*), aromatic lavender, rosemary, thyme and sage, laid out in a simple configuration of beds, it will be both functional and eye-catching.

Top *Houseleek is a useful plant for soothing skin irritations.*

Above *Pot marigolds are picked for drying before they have a chance to go over.*

Plan for an apothecary's garden

This garden of medicinal plants is based on the old idea of individual plots for each herb, but simplified and brought up to date by setting the herbs among paving slabs. The plan is uncomplicated by the need to lay paths, or put in edgings. All that is required is a level, completely weed-free site, some paving slabs and a base of sand and cement to bed them into. The design will fit a space of 4.5 x 6 m (15 x 19 ft).

Key to planting plan

1. *Calendula officinalis* – pot marigold – for soothing creams
2. *Sempervivum tectorum* – houseleek – for chapped skin and insect bites
3. *Myrtus communis* – myrtle – for sinusitis and bronchial infections
4. *Foeniculum officinalis* – fennel – for indigestion

5. *Marrubium vulgare* – horehound – for coughs
6. *Tanacetum parthenium* – feverfew – for migraines
7. *Salvia officinalis* – sage – for mouth and gum infections
8. *Lavandula stoechas* – lavender – for tension headaches
9. *Rosmarinus officinalis* – rosemary - for colds and depression

10. *Thymus vulgaris* – thyme – for sore throats
11. *Origanum onites* – pot marjoram – for arthritis
12. *Allium sativum* – garlic – for warding off colds
13. *Valeriana officinalis* – valerian – for insomnia
14. *Hypericum perforatum* – St John's wort – for anxiety and nervous tension

Boundaries

A herb garden with its own distinct boundaries becomes a secluded retreat, a place to sit and relax away from the pressures of the outside world. The key point is that the enclosing wall, fence or hedge does not have to be very solid, or even high – so as not to cast too much shade, which is usually better for gardens. It is the illusion of a place apart that counts, which can be achieved just as effectively with a low balustrade fence or plant-clothed pergola. And even a low division still provides some shelter, reduces the wind-chill factor and helps to retain and intensify the fragrance of the plants.

Above *A simple construction of posts and cross-rails divides areas of a kitchen garden.*

Above *Trelliswork, in the foreground, makes an effective internal division in a secluded garden bounded by a wall and plant-clothed walkway.*

A garden entirely enclosed by high brick walls enjoys its own warm microclimate. But in order not to be overpowering it has to cover a reasonably large area, as in the walled kitchen gardens of the grand houses of the past. In the smaller gardens of today, it is sometimes possible to make use of a high brick wall as one boundary, but other internal walls are best kept to a height of about 60 cm–1 m (2–3 ft).

Fences are a useful way to provide an instant screen and come in a wide range of materials. Choose one that is sympathetic to the overall style of your herb garden. A simple balustrade fence can work very well, or a traditional picket fence, popular in many American herb gardens: these are often painted white, but also look good with a green or blue finish. Wattle or wicker screens, as used in medieval enclosures, are another congenial fencing material.

Trelliswork, also known as treillage, makes a versatile boundary. It adds elegance and romance and works in formal or informal settings. Trellis comes in different patterns, may be painted in a range of colours and provides a frame for climbing plants. It is important, as for all fences, that the support posts are solid and firmly installed. The easiest and longest-lasting method of securing posts is to bed them into a custom-made pointed metal base set into the ground, or set them into a rubble and concrete base. Timber posts should be treated with preservative – choose one that does not harm plants. (If you use creosote, planting must be delayed for a year, as it can harm plants.)

Pergolas are another way of making a visual boundary, rather than a solid screen, and will suit a small garden as well as a large one. A covered or semi-covered walkway, clothed in plants, was a traditional feature of many 17th-century gardens and it was usually called an "arbour" or "herber". Strictly speaking a pergola should be constructed as a double row to form an arched walkway with a curved or rectangular top. But it can also be made as a single row of posts and cross-rails, to act as a support for climbers and to make an internal fence or division.

Espaliered fruit trees trained flat against a system of posts with wires strained horizontally between them provide an openwork, living screen as a boundary or division. They can be planted in a single row or a double one to form a walk. They also look good trained against a wall. Plant as young trees, removing any side shoots and training the branches along the wires as they grow.

Hedging Plants

Hedges make the ideal boundary for many herb gardens. They divide different areas and delineate paths. They may be formally clipped, or left to a more natural pattern of growth, and reach different heights to provide a high dense screen or a low division. Low, clipped hedges form knot-garden patterns. Choose from a selection of the following:

• *Taxus baccata* – Yew. Slow-growing, but makes a superb screen and its dark green provides a foil for many plants.

• *Buxus sempervirens* – Box. Makes an excellent hedge for a neat, clipped finish. Formal hedges – low to medium height.

• *Buxus sempervirens* 'Suffruticosa' – Dwarf box. Much more compact than the common box, ideal for knot gardens.

• *Santolina chamaecyparissus* – Cotton lavender. A silver plant which responds well to clipping into mounds or low hedges.

• *Teucrium chamaedrys* – Wall germander. The dark-green foliage needs frequent trimming to keep it in shape. Can be grown as an informal hedge and left to flower.

• *Origanum vulgare* 'Aureum' – Golden marjoram. Although it can be clipped to form mounds, its relaxed habit of growth makes it less suitable as a conventional formal hedge.

• *Rosmarinus officinalis* – Rosemary. Can be clipped to a squared-off hedge shape, or trimmed as an informal hedge.

• *Rosa rugosa* – Rose. This forms a dense, impenetrable barrier of medium to full height.

• *Artemisia abrotanum* – Southernwood. Light-green, feathery foliage makes a delightful informal hedge that needs trimming only once or twice a year.

• *Hyssopus officinalis* – Hyssop. It is possible to clip this to a formal shape, but the blue flower spikes make it worth growing in its natural form, lightly trimmed. Cut back in the spring.

• *Lavandula* spp. – Lavender. There are different heights to choose from. Makes a fragrant hedge, needing little attention, apart from cutting back firmly (but not into old wood) after flowering.

Planting a hedge

1 *Dig out a shallow trench along the line of the proposed hedge and fork over the soil at the base of it to ensure good drainage.*

2 *Add plenty of garden compost, digging it lightly into the soil, and just before planting, fork in a sprinkling of blood, fish and bone organic fertilizer, wearing gloves and a respirator mask.*

3 *Mark the centre line of the hedge with string and pegs, put in the plants, spacing them evenly by using a measured length of wood – 23 cm (9 in) apart is suitable for most. Fill in the soil, firming it around each plant, and water.*

4 *The hedge will soon become established, ready for its first trim in the second year. Give it a mulch of compost in subsequent years or add a little organic fertilizer to the soil, watering it in.*

Above *Rosemary forms a good hedge-like boundary in this enclosed herb garden.*

Focal Points

The design of the herb garden will be stronger and have more impact with the inclusion of focal points to draw the eye. They may be in a central position or at the end of a path or vista. A sundial is a traditional feature in many herb gardens. Birdbaths and fountains introduce the soothing element of water. A stone urn overflowing with trailing or flowering herbs is always a simple but effective centrepiece, and standard topiary trees in tubs make versatile and movable points of interest.

An arbour, in the sense of a covered seat or shelter, strikes just the right note in an ornamental herb garden. It provides a focal point as well as being a frame for climbing plants, and introduces the all-important dimension of height. At the same time it adds a hint of mystery and makes a secluded place to sit and enjoy the sights and scents of the surroundings. Sited at the end of a walk, in a far corner or high vantage point, it becomes an inevitable attraction that has to be visited. Arbours may be constructed from many types of materials including posts and rails, trellis, metal frames, or, for a more rustic look, wickerwork.

Archways can be sited to emphasize an important feature, such as a statue, within the garden itself, or to frame a distant view.

Right *The elegant façade of a distant house is framed by an archway of roses.*

Opposite *A fountain makes an attractive centrepiece in a sheltered garden.*

Below *A water-lily pond provides the focal point in the centre of a cloister herb garden.*

Choosing Herbs

When working out planting schemes it pays to think about the colour and texture of the herbs you choose and to group them for best effect. They will flourish and make a better show, too, if given the right conditions – damp or dry, sun or shade. One of the many advantages of a herb garden is that it has quite a long season of interest – often provided by the colour of the leaves (many of which are evergreen). Foliage colours available include silver, or silvery-blue, bronze, purple and gold as well as all the greens.

Ruta graveolens 'Jackman's Blue' – Rue. Steely-blue, strikingly indented foliage.
Salvia officinalis – Sage. Greeny-grey, oval, rough-textured leaves.
Santolina chamaecyparissus – Cotton lavender. A good strong silver, finely indented foliage.
Thymus vulgaris 'Silver Posie' and *T.* x *citriodorus* 'Silver Queen' – Best of the silver thymes, with delicate variegations.

Bronze and Purple

Ajuga reptans 'Burgundy Glow' – Bronze bugle. Glossy, bronze foliage.

Above *Rue and curry plant in flower.*

Silver

Artemisia abrotanum – Southernwood. Greeny-grey, feathery leaves.
Artemisia absinthium – Wormwood. Silvery-grey, finely indented leaves.
Artemisia ludoviciana 'Silver Queen' – Western mugwort. Fine, silvery lanceolate leaves.
Artemisia pontica – Roman wormwood. Silver, upright, foliage spikes.
Dianthus spp. – Pinks. Foliage colouring varies, most are blue-grey.
Eucalyptus globulus – Eucalyptus. Silvery-blue, smooth oval leaves, round when immature.
Helichrysum italicum – Curry plant. Silver, spiky leaf clusters.
Lavandula dentata var. *candicans* – Lavender. Woolly, finely toothed silvery-grey leaves.
Marrubium vulgare – Horehound. Greeny-grey, rounded, textured leaves.

Above Thymus x citriodorus *'Silver Queen'.*

Above *Feathery, bronze fennel.*

Atriplex hortensis 'Rubra' – Red orache. Purple-red, smooth, pointed leaves.

Foeniculum vulgare 'Purpureum' – Bronze fennel. Golden-bronze foliage.
Ocimum basilicum 'Dark Opal' – Purple basil. Glossy, purple leaves.
Ocimum basilicum 'Purple Ruffles' – Purple basil with purple, frilly leaves.
Salvia officinalis Purpurascens Group – Purple sage. Purple-green leaves.
Sambucus nigra 'Guincho Purple' – Purple-bronze elder with indented foliage.

Gold

Many of these are variegated, but the predominant effect is gold.

Above Origanum vulgare *'Aureum'.*

Buxus sempervirens 'Latifolia Maculata' – Golden box. Small golden leaves.
Laurus nobilis 'Aurea' – Golden bay. Smooth, oval golden leaves.
Melissa officinalis 'All Gold' – Golden lemon balm. Bright golden-yellow leaves, splashed with green.
Melissa officinalis 'Aurea' – Variegated lemon balm with gold and green leaves.
Mentha x *gracilis* 'Variegata' – Gingermint. Boldly patterned gold-and-green-striped leaves.
Origanum vulgare 'Aureum' – Golden marjoram. Yellow-gold, oval leaves.
Salvia officinalis 'Icterina' – Golden sage. Gold and grey-green variegation.
Thymus spp. – Thymes. Several of these have strong gold foliage. Among the best are *Thymus.* x *citriodorus* 'Archer's Gold', *T.* x *citriodorus* 'Aureus', *T.* 'Nitidus' and olive-green and gold *T.* 'Doone Valley'.

Above Mentha suaveolens 'Variegata'.

Variegated

Agave americana 'Variegata' – Agave. Yellow margins to spiky, blue-grey leaves.

Ajuga reptans 'Multicolor' – Bugle. Green, pink and cream variegated foliage.

Armoracia rusticana 'Variegata' – Variegated horseradish. A cultivar with striking, creamy-white stripes on green.

Mentha suaveolens 'Variegata' – Pineapple mint. Creamy-white margins to leaves.

Pelargonium crispum 'Variegatum' – Scented geranium. Crinkly, golden-edged leaves.

Pelargonium 'Lady Plymouth' – Scented geranium. Light-green leaves with creamy margins.

Ruta graveolens 'Variegata' – Variegated rue. Foliage dappled green and cream.

Salvia officinalis 'Tricolor' – Tricolor sage. Striking variegations of pink, greeny-grey and cream.

Above Ruta graveolens 'Variegata'.

Herbs with Colourful Flowers

Many herbs have colourful flowers which transform the garden when they are in bloom. Even those that do not have large flowers like their cultivated cousins, such as *Hypericum perforatum*, put on a good show in a mass planting.

Above *Red and white valerian with catmint.*

Ajuga reptans – Bugle. Blue flower spikes.

Alchemilla mollis – Lady's mantle. Frothy, greeny-yellow flowers.

Borago officinalis – Borage. Tiny, star-shaped flowers provide a mist of blue when planted en masse.

Calendula officinalis – Pot marigold. Brilliant, orange-yellow blooms.

Dianthus spp. – Pinks. Deep reds and pinks.

Helichrysum italicum – Curry plant. Bright-yellow button flowers.

Hypericum perforatum – St John's wort. Bright-yellow star-shaped flowers.

Hyssopus officinalis – Hyssop. Deep-blue flower spikes.

Inula helenium – Elecampane. Yellow, daisy-like flowers.

Lavandula spp. – Lavender. A range of misty-blues, mauves and purples.

Monarda didyma – Bergamot. There are many cultivars which come in a range of pink, red, purple and white.

Above *Sunflowers and nasturtiums.*

Nepeta x *faassenii* – Catmint. Mauve-blue flowers, spectacular in a mass planting.

Origanum onites, Origanum vulgare – Pot marjoram and oregano. Clusters of purple-red flowers.

Rosa spp. – Rose. Old-fashioned varieties have pink, red and white blooms.

Salvia officinalis – Sage. Massed purple-blue flower spikes.

Santolina chamaecyparissus – Cotton lavender. Bright yellow button flowers.

Thymus spp. – Many of the thymes have mauve to pinkish-red flowers.

Tropaeolum majus – Nasturtium. A range of bright yellows and oranges and a long-flowering season.

Above *Old-fashioned pinks (*Dianthus *spp.).*

Above *A variety of white-flowering herbs.*

Above *Bronze fennel and rosemary standing tall over a bed of low-growing herbs.*

Herbs with White Flowers

A garden of white-flowering herbs has a restful quality, especially if combined with silver-leafed plants and white and green variegated foliage. Many herbs have white flowers, others, such as borage, lavender and sage, have white-flowering forms. This is a selection:

Achillea millefolium – Yarrow. Small creamy-white umbels.
Allium tuberosum – Garlic chives. White star-shaped flowers.
Borago officinalis 'Alba' – A white-flowering borage.
Chamaemelum nobile – Chamomile. White daisy-like flowers.
Digitalis purpurea f. *albiflora* – White foxglove. Creamy-white spires.
Galium odoratum – Sweet woodruff. Small white stars.
Lilium candidum – Inimitable pure-white lilies.
Myrrhis odorata – Sweet cicely. Large white umbels.
Thymus serpyllum var. *albus* – A creeping, white-flowering thyme.
Valeriana officinalis – Valerian. Effective in a mass planting.

Right *Tall herbs – elecampane, fennel and a white-flowering goat's rue at the back of a border.*

Tall Herbs

When it comes to planning beds and borders it helps to know the eventual height and spread of plants. You can check the ultimate size of individual herbs in a good reference book, but the selection below are a reminder of "what not to put at the front". They are also useful for adding height to a scheme.

Angelica archangelica – Angelica. A classic for adding architectural impact.
Cynara cardunculus Scolymus Group – Globe artichoke. Earns a place in any scheme for the decorative value of its striking, purple heads.
Foeniculum vulgare – Fennel. A graceful feathery plant, which needs plenty of room.
Levisticum officinale – Lovage. Large clumps of glossy, green leaves need space to spread sideways and upwards.
Onopordum acanthium – Scotch thistle. The patterned leaves are relatively low-growing, but the flower stalks rise to a height of 2 m (6 ft 6 in).

Climbers

Another way to add the dimension of height to an otherwise flat design is by training creeping plants over arbours, archways, obelisks and twiggy tepees. Herbal creepers to choose from include:

Humulus lupulus – Hops. There are both green and golden-leaved varieties.

Jasminum officinale – Jasmine. This has star-shaped, perfumed white flowers in midsummer.

Lonicera periclymenum – Wild honeysuckle with creamy flowers, borne throughout summer. There are also many cultivars to choose from.

Rosa spp. *R. eglanteria* – Eglantine rose. Has very short-lived flowers. An old-fashioned climber, such as Mme Alfred Carrière, might be more rewarding. *R. gallica* 'Complicata' reaches 2 m (6 ft 6 in) and may be used as a pillar rose.

Top *Humulus lupulus 'Aureus'.*

Above *A bay tree with climbing roses.*

Above *Creeping thymes make effective and appealing ground cover.*

Ground-cover Herbs

For the front of a border, to fill an awkward corner, or as paths and lawns, ground-cover plants are invaluable.

Arctostaphylos uva-ursi – Bearberry. A mat-forming evergreen shrublet.

Chamaemelum nobile 'Treneague' – Non-flowering lawn chamomile. A non-flowering cultivar.

Juniperus communis 'Prostrata' – Juniper. Forms a dense, neat carpet, which no weed can penetrate.

Symphytum ibericum – Dwarf comfrey. A fast-spreading plant. Also comes in a gold-and-green variegated form.

Thymus serpyllum – There are many creeping thymes, ideal for paths, lawns and ground cover.

Vinca minor – Periwinkle. The dark-green leaves form dense, weed-defying cover. Cheerful blue flowers in spring.

Dry or Damp Soil?

It is usually easier to fit the plant to the right environment, rather than the other way about. Changing the soil and microclimate to accommodate a plant's particular preference can often be difficult and costly. The good news is that herbs are relatively easy-going plants and will often adapt to and grow well in conditions they would not choose in the wild. But to make things easier, it usually pays to give them what they want.

Dry, or certainly well-drained, soil suits the majority of plants, especially the shrubby herbs such as rosemary and thyme.

Damp-lovers to watch for include angelica, the *Mentha* genus and *Monarda didyma*. The mints and angelica will also grow happily in shade or semi-shade.

Herb Containers

Growing herbs in containers has many advantages. Where space is limited there is always room for a few pots, even in the smallest of gardens. Sited near the house, they provide the added convenience of being handy for harvesting – important for culinary herbs. As part of a garden scheme, containers can be placed in a bed to fill a temporary bare patch, used as focal points or arranged symmetrically to link different elements of a design.

Their mobility is a definite plus. Of course it must be borne in mind that very large pots, or those made of stone, will be too heavy to move. But, unlike static planting in a bed, small and medium pots, or those made of a lighter material, can be moved around to make a change. This is also useful for plants past their best, which need a less prominent position in which to recuperate. Tender and half-hardy herbs in containers can be moved under cover for winter protection.

Above *Comfrey has deep roots and needs a tall container (left back). Marjoram (centre) and thyme thrive in smaller pots.*

Planting

Growing a single species in a container gives plants room to develop and to provide plenty of leafy growth. For larger specimens, such as bay, sage and lemon verbena, it is essential that they do not

Above *Large pots planted with angelica add impact to a parterre.*

have to share a pot if they are to be left undisturbed for several years. The pot should be large enough to allow roots to spread. Mixed herb pots make very attractive features and are a good way of growing a variety of plants in a small space, but plants are inevitably cramped; roots become congested and annual replanting is usually necessary for a mixed planting.

Good drainage is one of the keys to success. Before you start, check that there is a large hole in the base of the pot, or several holes in the case of plastic pots and troughs. Put in a layer of crocks (broken terracotta pots), then cover with a layer of sand or grit (gravel) before filling with potting compost (soil mix).

Most herbs flourish in a free-draining environment and, as a general rule, a 3:1 mixture of soilless compost (planting mix) and loam-based compost (soil mix) gives the best results. For shrubby herbs, such as bay, sage and rosemary, and for scented pelargoniums, add a few handfuls of grit (gravel) to the mix to improve drainage. Do not be tempted to use garden soil; it will not provide enough nutrients and might harbour weeds and pests.

Maintenance

Extra fertilizer must be added after about four weeks, with subsequent weekly feeds throughout the growing season. An organic plant food based on seaweed extract is preferable, but slow-release fertilizer granules save time as they are added when potting up.

Pot-grown plants need frequent watering during the growing season. As a general rule, it is better to let them almost dry out and then give them a good soaking, rather than to keep dribbling in small amounts of water. Water-retaining gel mixed into the growing medium at the time of planting makes watering less of a chore. During the winter months pot-grown perennials should be given the minimum amount of water possible.

Plants that are kept in the same container for several years should have the top layer of compost, about 5 cm (2 in), scraped off and replaced with fresh every year. They will need re-potting in a container one or two sizes larger as roots become congested – try not to leave it until the plant is obviously suffering, with roots bursting out of the pot, yellowing leaves and poor, straggly growth.

Above *Herbs growing in separate pots with* Lavandula stoechas *at rear right.*

Planting a pot of mixed culinary herbs

1 *Mix slow-release fertilizer and water-retaining gel, following instructions, into a potting medium made up of 3:1 parts of soilless compost (planting mix) and loam-based compost (soil mix).*

2 *Put a layer of crocks (broken terra-cotta pots) in the bottom of the pot.*

3 *Fill to the first hole with the potting medium, settling it evenly.*

4 *Tap a plant out of its pot and feed it gently through the hole, working from the inside outwards.*

5 *Cover the roots with more compost and firm it down before adding a further layer of plants.*

6 *Put in more plants until all the holes are filled and finish with one or two plants on top. Water in thoroughly.*

YOU WILL NEED
Slow-release fertilizer; water-retaining gel; soilless compost; loam-based compost; trowel; terracotta pot; crocks (broken terracotta pots); a selection of culinary herbs

Right *Marjoram (top), alpine strawberry, thymes and parsley go well together in a pot of herbs for culinary use.*

Potting Composts

Potting composts (soil mixes) come in two main types: based on sterilized loam, and the soilless composts (planting mixes), based on peat or peat substitutes such as coir. Soilless composts are lighter and easier to handle, but they do not retain nutrients as long as the loam-based ones. They provide a more moist environment, but, if left unwatered, they also dry out more quickly, and are difficult to remoisten. Both types of potting compost are available containing nutrients in a range of proportions: "seed and cuttings" formula contains the least and a "potting" formula the most, with "all-purpose" in between.

Indoor Herb Gardening

Some herbs adapt well to being grown as houseplants. In regions with cold winters which suffer frosts, it is one way of cultivating tender herbs successfully. A conservatory gives scope for keeping a wider range, but is by no means essential. Give indoor plants as much natural light as possible and regular liquid feeds in summer, and do not overwater, especially in winter.

Vigorous and colourful, easy-to-grow scented pelargoniums are a rewarding group to grow this way as they come in such a variety of scents and leaf forms. Don't be afraid to prune them hard if they become straggly and never keep them too damp. Tender pineapple sage (*Salvia elegans*) does well indoors and produces scarlet flowers in late autumn or winter just when colour is welcome. It needs a big pot and more water than most. *Aloe vera* adapts well to an indoor regime, requiring the minimum of attention. A gritty, free-draining compost (soil mix) suits it best and infrequent but thorough watering. Myrtles do not always survive frosts and are another good choice. The dwarf *Myrtus communis* 'Tarentina', having a compact and tidy habit of growth, is eminently suitable, and *Myrtus communis* 'Variegata', being even less hardy, is well worth growing inside.

Herbs on the Windowsill

A supply of indoor culinary herbs is a great convenience. It is possible to grow them on the kitchen windowsill as long as you take into account the stress this puts on the plants. If you put a young plant into a small pot and then keep cutting off its leaves, it will be hard pressed to survive. At the same time, it is being kept short of air, the atmosphere may be too hot and steamy and changes of temperature extreme. From the point of view of flavour, there is little sun to bring out the essential oils.

The best way to counteract these problems is to alternate pots kept on the windowsill with another set left standing outside. Keep the different herbs in individual pots and group them together. They grow better in close proximity to one another because transpiration from the massed leaves increases the overall humidity.

Standing the pots on a gravel tray, or in a container with a layer of gravel on the base, keeps them cool and helps to retain moisture, without the plants becoming waterlogged.

Above *Herbs grouped together on the windowsill are handy for cooking.*

Far left *Scented pelargoniums and lemon verbena grow well as houseplants.*

Left *Culinary herbs in separate pots, standing in an outer container of gravel.*

Herbs in the Greenhouse

It is perfectly possible to grow many herbs without any form of winter protection or artificial heat. But in colder regions a small, frost-free greenhouse is a great help in extending both the season of growth and the range of plants it is possible to grow.

It is often easier to raise plants from seed sown in trays. Under controlled conditions, the success rate is usually higher. With a greenhouse you can start sowing much earlier than if you had to wait for the right outdoor conditions. But remember that young plants, grown on from seedlings, must be acclimatized gradually to being outside, before they are finally planted in the garden. Do this by standing them outside in the daytime for a short period, or transferring them to a cold frame.

Parsley is a good candidate for sowing under glass. Although it is reasonably hardy, it needs heat to germinate (about 18°C, 65°F), which is why it takes so long to emerge when planted straight into the garden early in the year before the soil has warmed up. Germination will be much quicker and more reliable if the seeds are started in trays in the greenhouse, with a view to transplanting outside once grown.

Basil is almost impossible to raise from seed in temperate regions without the benefit of glass. But it is not difficult to get good results if you follow a few guidelines:

• Do not start too early in the year; allow spring to get well under way first, when it will be easier to supply a temperature of 15–18°C (60–65°F).

• Scatter seeds as sparsely as possible, so that little thinning-out is required later and root disturbance minimized.

• Provide the seedlings with adequate ventilation and do not overwater to reduce risk of "damping-off" disease.

• Grow plants on in a large container, rather than planting them directly into the soil. They can then be kept outside or moved into a greenhouse, according to current weather conditions.

Above Capsicum frutescens *'Gipsy', in flower, in a greenhouse.*

Summer Herbs

Unless the summer is exceptionally cool and wet, sweet basil (*Ocimum basilicum*) will usually grow well in a pot outside, but the purple-leafed kinds seldom reach their full potential unless kept under glass.

Chilli peppers (*Capsicum* spp.) also need to be grown in the greenhouse in cooler climates if they are to produce mature, ripe fruits. In parts of the United States chilli peppers can be grown outside. Other herbs to try are the popular Japanese salad plants known as shiso (*Perilla frutescens* and *P. frutescens* 'Crispa') and the culinary flavouring plant, lemon grass, much used in Thai cookery (*Cymbopogon citratus*).

Adequate shading and copious watering are necessary for plants grown under glass in the summer.

Winter Protection

For container-grown plants that are not fully frost-hardy, such as bay, lemon verbena and myrtle, as well as more tender subjects such as scented pelargoniums, a cold greenhouse, provided it is frost-free, gives enough protection to keep them alive through the winter. In the summer months they can stand outside in the garden, as long as they are moved under cover before the first winter frosts.

Many of these plants will lose their leaves, even if they remain evergreen in warm climates. Once they have been moved into the greenhouse in the autumn, cut them back or trim lightly, according to individual requirements. Over the succeeding winter months give them a minimal amount of water and no fertilizer to ensure dormancy.

Growing Herbs

Once the design and overall style have been chosen, it is time to turn them into reality. Practical guidance is included in this chapter on how to do so, through the stages of planning and preparing the site, laying out paths and hard surfaces, to putting in the plants themselves. There are tips on successful propagation and how to train plants into standards or over frames. There is advice on maintenance and seasonal tasks, with a final section on dealing with pests and diseases.

Above *Tools of the trade in an old-style potting shed.*

Left *A supply of freshly cut material for recipes is one of the rewards of growing your own herbs.*

Planning Your Planting

Many of the most familiar herbs are Mediterranean in origin and grow best where there is plenty of sun. Bear this in mind when deciding on the location for your herb garden. Choose an area that has the sun for most of the day and where there is little dense or permanent shade. Take the time to watch the movement of the sun, so that you know exactly where shadows fall. This will help with planning the planting, allocating the right areas for herbs needing sun, shade or semi-shade and deciding where to site features such as a sundial, arbour, fountain or a seat. If you are at the survey stage in winter when the trees have no leaves, don't forget to take into account the deep shade cast by summer foliage.

Shelter is also important. Chilly winds, particularly in winter, can be devastating to many shrubby herbs such as thyme and rosemary. You may be able to make good use of an existing boundary wall to act as a windbreak. Consider putting in hedges, trelliswork or wicker fences to provide a sheltered, secluded environment, but remember that they will cause some shade and loss of light to plants. It may be better to install them on one or two sides only, according to prevailing wind direction, leaving other sides open or with low balustrade fencing.

If productivity is the main objective it is best not to overdo the number of low hedges, central features and dividing pathways, all of which will diminish the amount of space available for cultivation. Nevertheless, the plot can still achieve considerable charm if the production is arranged in an orderly fashion and by building in a feature or two that will add overall interest.

Top *A carefully planned bed, with silvery spokes of* Santolina chamaecyparissus *in a wheel of block planting.*

Right *Herbs flourish in a garden sheltered by a high brick wall.*

Soil and Site Preparation

Time spent preparing the site by improving the soil and eliminating weeds will be repaid many times over. This is not as daunting as it might seem. Improving the texture of the soil (though not weed elimination) applies only to the planting areas and does not have to be carried out where paths and hard surface areas are to be laid.

A light, free-draining soil is best for most herbs. It warms up quickly in spring and does not become as cold and waterlogged as heavy soil in winter. But if it is too porous, moisture and nutrients will be quickly leached away, resulting in a soil so poor and dry that few plants will flourish. Forking in organic matter – garden compost or leaf mould – will ensure better results. On heavy soil, if areas are inclined to become water-logged it is worth digging out trenches and filling them with rubble to form land drains. Chalk and sand both drain rapidly whilst clay retains moisture. The ideal is a crumbly loam which retains the right degree of water and nutrients.

Many herbs, including lavender, do not grow well in a heavy clay soil. One way to overcome the problem is to put

Above *A raised bed provides good drainage.*

in raised beds filled with loamy topsoil. But if you intend to plant straight into existing ground, once again it will be necessary to incorporate organic matter.

For a very heavy soil, the addition of plenty of coarse grit helps to open up the texture further. Double digging, though hard work, is the way to do this most effectively. Take out a trench to the depth of two spades at one end of the plot, turning it straight into a wheelbarrow and removing it to the other end of the area to be treated. Add a layer of grit and

compost to the first trench, covering it with soil from the next section. Continue in this pattern until the whole area has been dug over and organic matter incorporated. When the last trench is reached fill this with the soil from the first trench. After digging, tread down the soil lightly to ensure that no air pockets remain and that the soil does not subsequently settle unevenly. Rake over in several different directions until the surface is level and leave it for a week or so before planting.

Beware of overmanuring ground where herbs are to grow. The object of digging in bulky organic matter is to improve texture and drainage. For the majority of herbs, heavy feeding with rich farmyard manure or artificial fertilizers encourages soft growth, reduces aroma, and lays the plants open to attack by pests and diseases.

Another factor to consider is the alkaline or acid content of the soil, measured by the pH factor. A figure of seven is taken as neutral – anything higher is alkaline, anything lower is on the acid side. An inexpensive soil-testing kit will tell you what you have. Herbs are a disparate group, but as a rule most will grow in a neutral soil.

Weeding

Eliminating perennial weeds as thoroughly as possible before putting in plants pays great dividends. Another advantage of double digging is that you can take out deep roots and every speck of greenery you see as you go along. Fork out all weeds as painstakingly as possible. For stubborn or dense weed growth, cover the area for a full season with a layer of thick black polythene (plastic). Once this is removed, all but the most persistent weeds will be obliterated.

If you would rather get started on the planting immediately, put down a layer of black polythene (plastic), cut with holes for planting pockets, making sure these are completely weed free. Then put in the plants and cover the surface of the polythene with a mulch of gravel or bark chippings.

Above *Double digging eliminates weeds and improves soil texture.*

Above *Forking out weeds.*

Above *Removing all trace of roots helps keep the soil clear for longer.*

Laying Out a Garden

The first thing to do is to make a plan to fit your plot and requirements. You can take it from an existing design in a book, but you will need to tailor it to fit your own site. Check that you have the space to carry out your chosen scheme, that it will complement its surroundings and not be too cramped. Then measure the site and note the position of any existing walls, trees or other features that are to be kept.

Decide on a scale and draw up the plan on graph paper, but remember that it is all too easy to put in too much, too close together. It may look good on paper but will not work in reality. Keep checking as you go along that the layout you have drawn is feasible on site. The simpler it is and the fewer fussy elements you include, the more impact the finished garden is likely to have.

Marking Out a Garden

Once you have worked out the design and chosen the site, it is time to lay it out on your plot and put in hard surfaces.

Take your paper plan on to the chosen area and mark the key points on the ground with stakes. Designate the boundaries and outline the beds and paths with string and pegs, measuring carefully and ensuring that right angles are accurate with a builder's square. A length of garden hose is useful for marking out curves. At this stage it is possible to check that the proportions are right, that the whole scheme is well balanced and that other parts of the garden do not intrude or clash with the general concept. An upstairs window is often the best place to get a good overall view. Now is the time to change anything that does not look right – it will be difficult and costly to alter later on. It is best to decide on the order of work before you start:

• Changes of levels or major earthworks, including digging out ponds, need to be done first.

• Construction work, paths, terraces, hard surface areas, herb wheels and raised beds come next.

• Boundaries need to be clearly marked before you start, and, if putting in a wall, you may want to do this first, as well as putting in fence posts. But for ease of access and wheelbarrow movement it usually pays to leave fences till after the hard construction is done. Hedges, too, should be put in at a later stage with the bulk of the planting.

• Features such as pergolas, arbours and fountains may be put in at the same time, or after the hard-surface construction.

• Preparation of the soil in the beds should be done a few days in advance of planting if possible.

• Planting the herbs is practically the last stage.

• Finishing touches include adding container plants to the scheme and movable features such as sundials.

Above *Contrasting coloured stones, in this cobbled surface, pick out a star motif and decorative border.*

Putting in Paths and Hard Surface Areas

All paths and hard surface areas require a firm, level base. This can be done by marking a series of pegs with a line 5 cm (2 in) from the top. Hammer the pegs into the ground across the area to be levelled, tapping them in until the tops are flush with each other (using a spirit level to check). Then level and firm down the soil to the mark on the pegs.

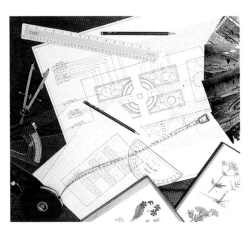

Above *Drawing out the design on paper helps to achieve a successful result.*

Above *A random pattern of paving stones.*

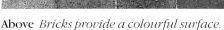

Above *Bricks provide a colourful surface.*

Gravel is a relatively inexpensive, quickly laid surface. It comes in a range of colours and in two main types: crushed stone from quarries and pea shingle (pea stone) from gravel pits. It should be laid on a level, well-compacted base of soil covered with a layer of dry concrete, eight parts ballast (gravel) mixed with one part cement, which has been left to dry off for several days. Hessian mesh (burlap), laid over the path before the gravel is spread, prevents weeds.

Stone slabs are a good surface for a terrace or large paved area. They are also useful for using as stepping stones in a wide border and for a mixed surface path of gravel and paving slabs. Bed them into mortar on a hardcore base (stones and broken bricks), as for the brick path, below.

Cobblestones are an attractive finish for a small scale area. They can be used to fill in round shrubs and trees or to lay in conjunction with other hard-surface materials. Pack them together as closely as possible, set in a bed of mortar on a hardcore base.

Bricks must be hard, impermeable and resistant to frost. Reclaimed bricks, from specialist merchants, have the best mellow colour. They must be laid on a firm, hardcore surface or they will expand and lift with the moisture in the soil and form an uneven path. For a path with less heavy wear a sand base without hardcore is sufficient.

To lay a main brick path

This construction will be suitable for main paths in a herb garden and should withstand average domestic use and weather conditions.

YOU WILL NEED
Timber boarding; wooden pegs; mallet; spirit level; hardcore (stones and broken bricks); ballast; cement; rake; hard, impermeable bricks (about 24 for an area 60 cm (2 ft) wide by 1 m (3 ft) long); sand, a large broom

1 *Dig out soil for the path to a depth of one brick plus 10 cm (4 in) for the base. Tread it down till level. Put in an edging of timber boards, held in place with hammered-in pegs, with their upper edges at the level of the finished path. Spread a 7.5 cm (3 in) layer of hardcore, rolling it in until firmly compacted.*

2 *Cover the hardcore base with a dry mix of eight parts ballast to one part cement, approximately 2.5 cm (1 in) thick, lightly tamp it with the head of the rake to fill in any gaps in the hardcore, and then rake to a loose, level surface.*

3 *Lay the bricks into the ballast and cement base, arranging them in a staggered pattern so that you don't have a line of joints. Tap each one down with a mallet, butting it as close to its neighbour as possible; check with a spirit level that the path is even in all directions as you go.*

4 *When all the bricks are in place, spread more ballast and cement over the surface, brushing it repeatedly into the joints to fill them, before cleaning off the surplus. Moisture from the soil will set the cement, but a light spray of water may be applied to hasten the process.*

5 *Before the cement hardens, ease sand from the joints to create pockets for prostrate herbs, then fill in with a little topsoil and sow seeds or plant divisions from established plants.*

Planting the Garden

Once you have a stock of established perennials you will be able to increase them by propagation, and many annuals and biennials will conveniently seed themselves. But you are sure to need to buy some plants in order to get your herb garden started.

Buying Plants

Specialist herb nurseries should have many of the more unusual varieties, but many garden centres now offer a reasonable selection. As you will require several of each species for a good show, the initial outlay could be considerable, so make sure you buy only strong, healthy specimens and follow these tips to get the most for your money:

• Check that a plant has not been too recently potted and whether it lacks a strong root system, or conversely that it has not been too long in the pot and the roots have become congested. Make sure there are no weeds, algae or moss.

• Examine the plant carefully for pests – red spider mite and whitefly may not be obvious at first glance.

• Don't buy anything with discoloured , wilting or blotched leaves – it could be diseased.

• Never assume that a stunted, straggly and overgrown or poor and sickly specimen will improve once planted out. It won't.

• Resist the temptation to buy annuals potted up singly. Many do not transplant well and seed quickly in hot, dry weather – these include coriander (cilantro), chervil, dill and borage. Grow them yourself from seed. Once established they often self-seed.

• Look for annual flowering herbs, such as pot marigolds and nasturtiums, sold as bedding plants in trays, rather than in single pots – or grow them yourself from seed.

• It will probably be necessary to thin seedlings to give them room to develop; and keep them well weeded to prevent competition for moisture and nutrients.

Planting the Design

If you have drawn in the herbs on your plan, this can be very useful as a guideline. A pre-designed scheme helps to group plants effectively for colour, texture, height and so on. However, it is not always easy to visualize on paper how it will look on the ground. Standing the plants in their pots on the soil, and shifting them around as necessary, helps with spacing and final decisions on position which often leads to a happier end result. It cannot be stressed enough that plants always look best in groups, rather than being scattered about singly. A whole bed of purple sage makes a

Above *One healthy and one poor container-grown vervain plant.*

Top *A well-stocked herb garden.*

much more dramatic statement than one little clump lost in a mass of competing colour. A broad sweep of catmint or borage is a sight to savour.

The same principle applies to climbers grown over an arched walkway. With several different plants the result can be very haphazard. One variety will have impact.

Invasive Herbs

Be careful where you put invasive plants. Comfrey, horseradish, sweet cicely and other herbs with strong tap roots can be very difficult to eradicate if you later want to change the planting scheme.

Some herbs, particularly those with creeping roots, encroach on their neighbours. Mint is a well-known culprit; soapwort and tansy can also prove overpowering. It is best to confine them with divisions in the bed: bricks or tiles buried in the soil work very well for shallow-rooting invasive herbs.

Another way to curtail them is to grow them in a large container buried in the soil – but make sure it has adequate drainage holes, or the base removed, if the plants are not to become choked.

Planting a herb garden

1 *When you have put in all the hard surfaces in your garden and prepared the soil as necessary (see Soil and site preparation) it is time to plant up the scheme. Fork in a little organic fertilizer first, to give your herbs a good start, but avoid heavy manure.*

2 *Always water plants well in their pots first, as plants never take up moisture as well after planting if put in dry. Add water until it trickles out of the base of the pot – this is important for trees, shrubs and larger specimens, which may look damp on top but are dry at the rootball.*

3 *Mark your planting positions with sand. Tap each herb out of its pot, make a hole with a trowel, and put in the plant, firming the soil lightly around it afterwards. Water in well. Under very dry conditions it helps if you fill the planting hole with water first.*

4 *Keep the area free of weeds so that the newly set out herbs do not have to compete for moisture and nutrients.*

YOU WILL NEED

Garden fork; organic fertilizer; a selection of herbs; watering can; trowel; sand

Right *Recently planted aromatic herbs, set out in a knot pattern, surround a dwarf standard tree.*

Propagation

Propagating your own herbs is a rewarding occupation and the best way to replace plants and to stock your garden economically. The basic techniques are not difficult, but, as herbs are such a disparate range of plants, their requirements and the degree of difficulty in raising them varies. Some are much easier to propagate than others. Many respond better to one method than another so check for the optimum propagation method for each plant.

Raising from Seed

Many herbs are easy to grow from seed. Spring is generally the best time for sowing, but do not start too early: seeds sown when air and soil temperatures are warmer and light levels higher will grow into stronger plants. Some seeds are sown in autumn, as indicated here.

Annuals: All annuals – plants whose life cycle is completed in one year – can be grown from seed sown in spring. Hardy annuals, such as chervil (*Anthriscus cerefolium*), coriander (cilantro) (*Coriandrum sativum*) and pot marigold (*Calendula officinalis*) may also be sown in autumn to give them an early start the following spring. Half-hardy annuals, such as nasturtiums (*Tropaeolum* spp.), should not be sown until late spring or early summer in areas where there is frost. Basil (*Ocimum basilicum)* is tender and should be sown in seed trays under glass in late spring to early summer.

Biennials: These are planted in the late summer or early autumn of one year, to flower the following year – though some of them go into a third year, their life cycle is over once they have flowered. Although parsley is a biennial, it is worth sowing seed every year because the stems coarsen and it does not produce such good leaf in its second year. Biennials include angelica (*Angelica archangelica*), caraway (*Carum carvi*), clary sage (*Salvia sclarea*) and evening primrose (*Oenothera biennis)*.

Perennials: These live for a number of years and many perennial herbs can be successfully raised from seed. But not all of them produce seed, such as French tarragon (*Artemisia dracunculus*) and the non-flowering golden sage (*Salvia officinalis* 'Icterina'). Many hybrids and cultivars do not come "true" from seed, which means they may vary considerably from the parent plant. This includes all the mints, most lavenders and ornamental thymes. These must be vegetatively propagated.

Vernalization: A few herb seeds need to be subjected to a period of intense cold before they will germinate. In the wild, this ensures their survival where winters are cold. To reproduce these conditions artificially, in a process known as "vernalization" or "stratification", put the seeds in a polythene (plastic) bag of moist sand and leave in a refrigerator or freezer for 4–6 weeks before sowing.

This is necessary for: aconitum or monkshood (*Aconitum napellus*), arnica (*Arnica montana*), agrimony (*Agrimonia eupatoria*), juniper (*Juniperus communis*), hawthorn (*Crataegus laevigata*), *Primula* spp., *Rosa* spp., sweet cicely (*Myrrhis odorata*), sweet woodruff (*Galium odoratum*) and sweet violet (*Viola odorata*).

Scarification: Some hard-coated seeds, such as those of legumes, which include broom, clovers and vetches, will germinate more readily if first rubbed with fine sandpaper. This breaks up the outer coating and allows moisture to penetrate, which all seeds require before they will germinate.

Left *Careful labelling prevents misidentification when new seedlings emerge.*

Sowing in seed trays

The success rate for seeds sown in trays under controlled conditions is higher than for seeds sown outdoors. It is the best method for very fine seeds, such as parsley, and essential for raising tender plants, such as basil. It is also a good way to give many plants an earlier start.

YOU WILL NEED

Cellular seed tray; soilless seed and cuttings compost (soil mix); watering can; herb seeds; garden sieve; label; polythene (plastic) dome or plastic bag; 7.5 cm (3 in) pots

---

1 *Fill a seed tray with soilless growing medium. A tray divided into cells makes it easier to sow thinly and to pot up seedlings with minimum root disturbance. Water first, then scatter two or three seeds in each compartment.*

2 *Cover the tray with a layer of sieved compost (soil mix). Never bury seeds too deeply, especially small ones such as parsley. Water again and don't forget to label the tray (tiny seedlings look similar).*

3 *Put a polythene (plastic) dome over the tray, or enclose it in a plastic bag, to retain moisture. Put the tray on a windowsill or in the greenhouse until the seedlings emerge.*

4 *When the seedlings come through remove the cover and put the tray in a light place out of direct sunlight. Keep moist, but never waterlogged.*

5 *As soon as the seedlings are large enough to handle, pot them up in 7.5 cm (3 in) pots filled with fresh potting compost (soil mix). When strong and bushy they can be planted out.*

Sowing Outdoors

Many seeds can be sown outdoors directly into the soil where they are to grow, or in nursery beds for later transplantation. It is also the sensible way to raise herbs that do not respond well to being transplanted. These include coriander (cilantro), chervil and dill. It is as well to remember that there is a higher failure rate for seeds sown outdoors, rather than in a tray in the greenhouse, due to unexpected adverse weather conditions or the unwanted attention of birds or rodents. On the other hand it saves time and energy in pricking out, potting up and hardening off, and plants raised this way are often sturdier. For a good chance of success with outdoor seeds:

• It is best not to start too early in spring, if still cold. But to speed things up cover the area with cloches for a week or two in advance of sowing to warm up the soil.

• First weed the area thoroughly and rake it to a fine texture and level surface.

• Next make a shallow depression with a stake, or rake handle, in the soil and sprinkle in seeds as thinly as possible. Larger seeds, like nasturtiums or coriander (cilantro) can be placed individually rather than scattered.

• Cover seeds with a thin layer of soil, patting it down lightly, but beware of burying them too deeply.

• Don't forget to mark the area planted clearly. Sowing in straight lines, as appropriate for producing some culinary herbs, makes it easier to distinguish seedlings from weeds.

• Water well after planting and keep the area moist until the seedlings appear.

Above Calendula officinalis *grown from seed.*

Germination Requirements

For seeds to germinate successfully they require:

Moisture: The surface of the growing medium in seed trays must not be allowed to dry out, and outdoor seeds need frequent watering in dry spells.

Warmth: Most seeds need some degree of warmth to germinate, though temperature requirements can vary considerably. Most plants native to northern Europe and North America germinate at 10–13°C (50–55°F); plants from tropical and southern latitudes 15–21°C (60–70°F). Those herbs with special requirements include: lavender, exceptionally low at 4–10°C (40–50°F), parsley, 18–21°C (65–70°F), and rosemary, especially high at 27–32°C (80–90°F).

Light: Seeds should not be sown too deeply, in order that light may penetrate the soil and waken the seed into growth. This is particularly important for fine seeds – larger ones can be buried a little deeper. Light is crucial for thyme (*Thymus vulgaris*), winter savory (*Satureja montana*), poppies (*Papaver* spp.) and also sweet marjoram (*Origanum majorana*).

Air: A peat-based (or peat-substitute) growing medium is best for seeds, as the open texture allows air to circulate and oxygen to reach the developing plant. This is why breaking up the soil to a fine tilth is necessary for outdoor sowing and why seeds fail in compacted, water-logged soil.

Vegetative Propagation

Many perennial herbs are best propagated vegetatively, rather than by seed. This includes those that do not flower and set seed.

Above *Mint (in pot) grown from cuttings.*

Taking cuttings from the stems during the growing season is an effective method for many. Softwood cuttings are taken from soft, new growth in spring through to midsummer. They root quickly with warmth and humidity. Suitable for: *Origanum* spp., *Pelargonium* spp., *Santolina* spp., *Tanacetum* spp., *Mentha* spp. and *Salvia elegans*.

Semi-ripe cuttings are taken from harder, half-ripened wood in mid to late summer and can be taken from many shrubby herbs, including *Buxus* spp., *Citrus* spp., *Helichrysum italicum*, *Rosmarinus officinalis*, *Thymus* spp., *Lavandula* spp. and *Myrtus* spp. Some plants, including *Salvia elegans* and *Artemisia abrotanum*, root from stem cuttings taken at any time during the growing season.

Hardwood cuttings are taken from mature wood in mid to late autumn. They are slow to root (up to 12 months), and are usually kept in a cold frame over winter. This is suitable for trees, shrubs and roses.

Stem cuttings

Many herbs, such as rosemary and southernwood, are best propagated from cuttings. It is also the only way to perpetuate a special flower colour, such as pink-flowered hyssop, or a leaf variation, such as variegated rue. Stem cuttings are all taken in the same way. Do not cram in too many cuttings or put one in the middle of the pot.

YOU WILL NEED

Plants; sharp knife or secateurs (pruners); polythene bag; hormone rooting powder; 15 cm (6 in) pot; cuttings compost (growing medium); dibber (dibble), pencil or stick; plastic dome or bag

1 *Collect only a small amount of material at a time and be sure to keep in the shade in a polythene bag, to minimize water loss. Choose sturdy, non-flowering stems, with lots of leaves. Cut a section about 10 cm (4 in) just below a leaf joint and remove all but the top two or three leaves. These are necessary to supply the plant with nutrients as the root system develops.*

2 *Dip the cuttings into hormone rooting powder, tapping off any excess, and insert them into holes made with a dibber (dibble) round the edge of a pot filled with moist cuttings compost (growing medium). Water lightly and cover with a plastic dome or polythene bag held over a wire frame and sealed at the bottom – this is to maintain maximum humidity.*

3 *Once the cuttings have rooted – 2–4 weeks for softwood cuttings, 4–6 weeks for semi-ripe cuttings – repot into new compost and harden them off gradually before planting out.*

Root cuttings

A method of increasing herbs with creeping roots, such as mint (*Mentha* spp.), soapwort (*Saponaria officinalis*), bergamot (*Monarda didyma*) and herbs with taproots such as horseradish (*Armoracia rusticana*).

YOU WILL NEED

Garden fork; mint, or other suitable plant; secateurs (pruners); seed tray; cuttings or all-purpose compost (growing medium); watering can

1 *Lift a root of mint and cut it into 4 cm (1½ in) pieces. Try to cut at a point where there is a small bud from which a new plant can grow.*

2 *Fill a seed tray with cuttings compost. Lay the pieces of root on the surface, press them in and cover with a further layer of compost. Water and leave in a shady place. There is no need to cover the tray or enclose it in polythene, but do keep it moist.*

3 *Once there are plenty of leaves showing through, divide the new plants and grow them on in bigger pots or plant them out in the open ground.*

Division of roots

Herbs with fibrous or fleshy taproots are very easy to propagate by division. These include: chives (*Allium schoenoprasum*), oregano (*Origanum* spp.), lemon balm (*Melissa officinalis*), lovage (*Levisticum officinale*) and comfrey (*Symphytum* spp).

1 *Dig up a clump of chives. Divide it into several new pieces, pulling it apart with your hands or the aid of a small fork if necessary.*

2 *Cut off some of the top growth. Replant in open ground or firm each new piece into a pot filled with all-purpose compost.*

3 *Keep the new plants well watered. They will soon grow strongly to provide plenty of fresh leaf.*

Layering

A useful method of propagation for shrubby herbs such as bay, rosemary and sage. It works by inducing a side stem to develop new roots while still attached to the parent plant. Mound layering is particularly suitable for thymes, which become straggly after a few years. Pile gritty loam in a mound over the lower, leafless stems, leaving the crown of the plant showing. This stimulates new roots to develop at the base, when they can be separated and then planted in a different position.

1 *Trim the lower leaves from a side stem, attached to the shrub. Bend it over and bed into soil beside the plant.*

2 *Fasten it down with a staple or peg. Water in and leave for several months until roots have formed. Divide the new plant from the parent and replant it.*

Maintenance

Herbs are easy-going plants. Most are not difficult to grow, coming up year after year, or self-seeding exuberantly; but a herb garden, like any other garden, needs regular care and maintenance to keep it looking at its best. Keeping paths and gravel areas free of weeds makes all the difference to the overall appearance, especially in formal gardens, which depend on symmetry and orderliness for effect. If you don't like using weedkiller, there is nothing for it but to hoe out offenders as soon as you see them. Try not to let weeds seed or else the problem will be compounded.

Mulching is a good way to keep beds and borders weed-free. Use well-rotted garden compost, mushroom compost, leaf mould or bark chippings and pile it on thickly round plants. Weeds that come up through the mulch will be weak and easy to pull out. Gravel is also a suitable mulch and weed suppressant for thymes and many shrubby herbs. Grass clippings are useful for mulching round fruit bushes and the base of trees – they can be used fresh, added in a thick layer and allowed to rot down. For weeds with persistent roots, spreading heavy-duty black polythene (plastic) over the area for a full season helps to eradicate them by depriving the seedlings of light and air.

Deciding which plants are un-desirable is not always straightforward, as plenty of herbs are wild plants and often described as "weeds". You may decide to keep some self-sown plants, either leaving them in situ or transplanting to a more convenient spot, and this can add to the interest of the garden. The main thing is to be in control and not to let unwanted plants take over and dominate the scheme.

Clipping

In a formal scheme keeping plants clipped is all-important. Some will need cutting only twice a year, but others may require more frequent light trims to keep them in shape.

Many herbs grow prolifically, if left to themselves, and need frequent cutting back if the garden is not to become untidy and overgrown. Pruned plants can often be harvested for culinary or household use and any spares should be added to the compost heap. Spring is a good time to do some initial tidying and trimming, but many plants will need further cutting back during the summer months or in autumn.

Watering

It should not be necessary to give extra water to fully grown herbs planted out in the garden, except under severe drought conditions. Many of the shrubby herbs of Mediterranean origin are resistant to a shortage of water – rosemary flourishes in the driest of summers. But moisture-lovers, such as angelica, bergamot and mint, may need some help at these times. And of course it is essential in dry spells to water newly planted young herbs until they are well-established.

Mulching often helps to conserve moisture, but if it is to be effective for this purpose it must be added early in the season before the soil dries out.

The main task is to water container-grown herbs throughout the growing season. In their dormant period, during winter, they should be kept barely moist, or root rot may ensue.

Feeding

Although it is important to keep the soil "in good heart" with the addition of garden compost, heavy manuring and fertilizing with high-nitrogen inorganic products is to be avoided. It results in soft, sappy growth which is susceptible to blackfly infestation and will not withstand the stress of droughts or extreme cold. Worst of all the herbs will lack fragrance and aroma.

A slow-release organic fertilizer, such as blood, fish and bone, forked into the soil, helps to get new plants off to a good start. And any fruit and vegetables in the herb garden will require extra nourishment in the form of liquid seaweed or a comfrey fertilizer. Container-grown plants benefit from regular liquid feeds throughout the growing season, especially older plants that have been in the same pot for some time.

Above *A standard bay in a tub needs regular clipping with secateurs (pruners) and feeding.*

Opposite *A rotting compost heap.*

Above *A meticulously maintained garden.*

Comfrey Fertilizer

Comfrey is invaluable as a herb garden fertilizer, containing all the nutrients necessary for healthy plant growth in digestible form. It has a high potash content and is also a source of nitrogen, phosphorus and many other elements. Use it in the following ways:

• As a mulch by spreading freshly cut comfrey leaves round plants (blackcurrants and other fruit bushes benefit particularly). Topping the comfrey with a layer of lawn mowings adds bulk and speeds decay.

• Add comfrey leaves to the compost heap in thin layers – it doesn't add to the humus content, but works as an "activator", encouraging the breakdown of other plant material. Be careful to avoid adding roots and flowering stems, which will regenerate and form unwanted plants.

• As a liquid fertilizer, by filling a bucket to the halfway mark with comfrey leaves, fill it with water and cover with a lid – to exclude insects. Leave for 4–5 weeks, then strain off the liquid (which will be very smelly) and use it undiluted as an organic fertilizer for container plants, tomatoes and general garden use.

• A more concentrated version may be made by standing a bucket with a hole in the bottom over another container, filling the bucket with comfrey leaves and pressing them down with a weighted board. The bucket should then be covered with a lid and the leaves left to rot down for several weeks, until a black, tarry liquid seeps out. This should be diluted in water before use.

Above *A variety of garden clippings and fresh vegetable material is added to the heap, for a good supply of garden compost.*

Making a Compost Heap

A good supply of garden compost is always needed in the herb garden for improving the structure and fertility of the soil and as a mulch material.

Containers: There are many types of manufactured compost bins available in plastic, wood and other materials, suitable for gardens of varying sizes, but you can easily make your own. Build the heap straight on to the earth, with a surround of wire mesh, or timber boards to contain it. If using boards, leave airspaces between them.

Materials: Any plant material is suitable, such as, leaves, flowers, lawn clippings, straw, vegetable peelings. Woody stems should be included only if they have been mechanically shredded. Do not add difficult-to-eradicate perennial weeds, especially with their roots or main flowering stems attached. Annual weeds are best avoided if there is any chance of their seeding.

Construction: Build up the heap in layers, alternating lawn clippings with leaves and open-textured material – a variety of materials leads to a better texture. Add an activator every two or three layers – a sprinkling of chicken manure, seaweed meal, blood, fish, and bone, or comfrey leaves.

Processing: Covering up the heap with polythene (plastic), or a manufactured lid helps conserve moisture, so that the heap rots more rapidly. It is not usually necessary to "turn" the heap if it has been well constructed, but it does help to break up material added in clumps, such as lawn mowings. It will take 3–6 months to achieve a dark colour and moist crumbly texture.

Management: Have at least two heaps simultaneously at different stages of decay – one being for current use and one under construction. Dig out the compost from the bottom so that the old material is used first.

Spring Tasks

Propagating and planting are key tasks in what is the busiest and probably most exciting time of the year in the herb garden, with everything burgeoning into new growth. But the timing of "spring" varies greatly from one area to another and from one year to the next, so always take local conditions into account when carrying out suggested tasks.

Propagating

Early spring is the time for sowing seeds of hardy annuals in trays in a cold greenhouse, including borage, summer savory and pot marigold. You can also sow parsley if you can provide constant heat for germination; and perennials that are easy to raise by this method include fennel, sage (*Salvia officinalis* only), pot marjoram, winter savory and horehound. Of the thymes, only common thyme (*Thymus vulgaris*) and wild thyme (*T. serpyllum*) can be grown from seed. Others, which are cultivars, have to be vegetatively propagated.

Leave annuals such as basil, sweet marjoram and nasturtium until late spring, when they can be grown on outside without danger of frost. Seeds of herbs that dislike being transplanted should be sown outside, where they are to grow, including dill, chervil and coriander (cilantro).

Hardy annuals and perennials that are easy to raise from seed should not be sown outdoors until later in spring, when the soil has warmed up.

Now is the time to take root cuttings of mint, tarragon, bergamot and chamomile. There is no need to provide any extra heat.

To layer herbs, mound up earth around straggly thymes and sages, to encourage new shoots, or bed a single branch into soil until it roots to form a new plant.

Fibrous-rooted herbs and herbaceous plants can now be divided throughout the spring months to make vigorous new plants.

Care of Seedlings

Seedlings raised in trays will have to be pricked out and potted up into 7.5 cm (3 in) pots, to develop and harden off before they are finally planted out in the garden.

Outdoor seedlings need thinning out, so that the plants left have enough space to grow and thrive. This is the best time, once the weather has warmed up a little and the soil is still moist, for planting out pot-grown herbs bought from the nursery.

Weeding

Hoe weeds and unwanted plants out of paths and beds immediately as they appear. They will be much easier to control if they are not allowed to set seed or grow too big, especially those with strong taproots. Spread mulch now to suppress weeds and conserve moisture. A mulch is most effective when soil is damp.

Preparing Soil

Prepare beds for planting by forking over and incorporating garden compost or slow-release fertilizer. In heavy soils dig in manure or bulky organic material.

Pruning

Be careful not to start pruning hard too early in spring when frosts are still likely. This is because it will stimulate plants into new growth, which will be susceptible to frost injury. As soon as the weather is suitable and all risk of frost is over, prune shrubs and silvery herbs that have suffered winter damage back to new shoots. Cut out dead and straggly growth on sages and thymes, but trim thymes only lightly, after flowering, as they do not respond well to heavy pruning. Rosemary can be cut back quite hard, but leave it until it has flowered. Trim box hedges, bays and all formal topiary shapes.

Containers

Trim out any dead or old growth on container-grown plants and start to give them more water and a liquid feed. Replant if necessary into a large pot with fresh growing medium.

Above *Lemon balm (*Melissa officinalis*) ready for dividing and replanting.*

Above *Clipping a santolina hedge.*

Above *Seedlings and overwintered cuttings.*

Summer Tasks

Now is the time to enjoy the garden, when plants are in bloom and looking their best. It is also the time for harvesting and making use of the bounty available.

Propagating

Stem cuttings can be taken from many plants, starting with softwood cuttings from late spring to midsummer and continuing with semi-ripe cuttings from late summer to early autumn.

Above *Taking cuttings of purple sage.*

Collect seeds of annuals as they ripen, for use, or for sowing to produce a new crop, such as poppies, pot marigolds, nasturtiums, sunflowers, dill and coriander (cilantro); and of biennials and perennials, including angelica, caraway, sweet cicely (*Myrrhis odorata*), fennel and lovage. Clean the seeds, removing the seed husks, and store in clearly marked paper envelopes. Do not store in polythene (plastic), as moisture will form and they will rot or start into growth. Seeds should be sown within a year of collection, and angelica must be sown within a few months as the seed soon loses viability.

Weeding and Watering

Continue a routine of diligent weeding, to prevent anything undesirable becoming established. Allow plants to self-seed as appropriate; some can always be transplanted. Top up mulches as necessary. Water newly planted herbs well and any moisture-lovers that may be suffering from drought. Water containers daily.

Above *Nasturtium seeds are collected for drying and sowing the following year.*

Harvesting and Pruning

Summer is the time to make maximum use of fresh-cut herbs in the kitchen and to harvest leaves for drying for winter use, as it is best to cut them before they come into flower. Leafy herbs, such as lovage and mint, should be cut down to ground level in early summer to midsummer, before they start to seed, in order to ensure a second crop. In very dry spells, watering may be needed to achieve this. Cut back chive flowers and stems for new leafy growth and dead-head roses and annuals to encourage new blooms. Cut aromatic foliage and flowers for drying to make pot-pourri.

For plants with variegations, such as variegated lemon balm, cutting out any stems that have reverted to all green helps to prevent the whole plant reverting. Variegated plants are mutants and less prolific in habit than the common version from which they were derived and if left alone the stronger-growing plain foliage will soon take over the whole plant.

Trim fast-growing herbal hedges, such as wall germander (*Teucrium chamaedrys*) and cotton lavender (*Santolina chamaecyparissus*), as often as necessary to keep them in shape during the growing season.

Above *If planting young herbs in summer, choose a damp spell and water well.*

Autumn Tasks

This is the season for clearing up and cutting back, preparing plants for dormancy and planning their protection through the colder months of winter. But there is still propagation to be done, too, if next year's garden is to fulfil its potential.

Propagating

Sow seeds of biennials, including angelica, clary sage (*Salvia sclarea*), anise and caraway in pots to keep in a cold frame or in a cold greenhouse over the winter. Seeds that require vernalization before they will germinate should be sown outdoors, either in pots or in the ground, including sweet cicely (*Myrrhis odorata*), aconite (*Aconitum napellus*), primrose (*Primula* spp.) and sweet violet (*Viola odorata*). The advantage of sowing in pots is that the seeds are less likely to disappear than if they were sown into the ground to be eaten by birds or to be washed away. Finish collecting seed heads for saving, as they ripen.

Above *Pot up French tarragon to encourage new shoots to appear in spring.*

Many perennials may be divided in autumn for replanting in the border or for starting off as new plants in pots. Dig up French tarragon, put it into a large pot and leave in the cold greenhouse over the winter, for dividing into new plants in spring.

Above *Hardwood rose cuttings.*

Hardwood cuttings of fully mature wood may be taken from shrubs and trees suitable for propagation by this method, including roses, blackcurrants and willow.

Clearing

Cut back dead top growth of hardy herbaceous perennials, which do not need winter protection, such as mint, lemon balm and pot marjoram. If left until spring, new growth is likely to come through before the old stems have been cut back, by which time it is difficult to cut them low enough without clipping into fresh, new foliage. Dig up and compost annuals, including pot marigold, borage, summer savory, sweet marjoram, and biennials in their second year, such as parsley and caraway.

Remove fallen leaves (to make compost or leaf mould) and garden debris – decaying material left lying on plants encourages fungal diseases.

Above *Remove annuals that have finished flowering.*

Pruning

In early autumn, well before the onset of frosts, give box hedges and formally clipped topiary a last trim. Many deciduous shrubs are pruned when they lose their leaves in late autumn to early winter. Common elder (*Sambucus nigra*) and its ornamental cultivars benefit from hard pruning at this time to encourage bushy new growth for the next season and to help retain a neat and controlled shape.

Soil Preparation

For new plantings, dig heavy soils and spread with manure to be broken down by winter frosts.

Above *Double digging the soil.*

Containers

Bring in tender and half-hardy container-grown plants before frosts begin. Cut back excess top growth and give them a minimal amount of water.

Plant Protection

Protect the crowns of French tarragon left in the ground, and other garden-grown plants that are not fully frost-hardy, with agricultural fleece or a coat of straw or bracken.

Dig up at least one tarragon root, to ensure its survival, and also tricolour sage and other less than hardy plants. Pot them up in John Innes compost (soil mix) or similar, and put them in a cool greenhouse to spend the winter.

Winter Tasks

During the cold months, when there is less to do outside, take stock of current schemes and plan for the year ahead. In many ways this is the start of the gardening year. Cleaning equipment ready for the new season will be instrumental when it comes to getting an early start on the springtime propagating programme. Order new seed catalogues in good time and plan new garden layouts.

Above *Order seed catalogues and choose seeds for the next season.*

Propagating

If you have a greenhouse, even an un-heated one, it is possible to force some herbs for an early crop. Mint and chives are ideal for this treatment. Dig up the roots in late autumn to early winter, divide and replant in a peaty growing medium in quite large pots. Tarragon will need some heat to bring it on early, but may be treated the same way. Plant trees, bare-rooted roses and hedges, such as hawthorn, during their dormant period, and plant garlic bulbs.

Above *Planting a beech hedge.*

Cleaning

Thoroughly wash and clean pots, seed trays and equipment for propagation, getting rid of scum and tidemarks (water stains). Clean out the greenhouse, wash the glass, and do not leave old bags of potting compost (soil mix) around to harbour pests and diseases. Oil and clean garden tools and equipment.

Above *Thoroughly clean pots before storing them until the spring.*

Construction

Provided the weather is not too severe, new paths, terraces or hard surface areas may be constructed, garden schemes laid out and beds prepared for planting. But heavy rain and frosts are not conducive to this work, so local conditions must be taken into account.

Containers

Protect terracotta and stone pots that have not been put under cover against severe temperatures by wrapping them in fleece or hessian. Roots of even relatively hardy plants are more vulnerable if grown in a container, and if the soil freezes it will expand, which is likely to crack the pot.

Give indoor container-grown plants the minimum of water, just enough to ensure the compost (soil mix) does not dry out completely, and do not feed.

Plant Protection

Check that outdoor-grown perennials, which are not totally hardy, such as lemon verbena (*Aloysia triphylla*) are adequately protected with fleece. Some of the ornamental thymes, such as *Thymus vulgaris* 'Silver Posie', will also benefit greatly from a light covering as they dislike cold winds and water-logged roots.

Above *Tying in branches to protect them from the weight of the snow.*

Above *Protecting a plant for the winter.*

Above *A polythene (plastic) plant cover.*

Topiary and Training

Shrubs and trees clipped into geometric shapes have been a garden feature since Roman times. They introduce an appearance of order and formality to the herb garden and provide a contrast for the exuberant growth of many of the other plants. Grown in a pot as a standard, one plant alone makes an interesting focal point, and several placed at strategic intervals lend unity to a scheme. Standards may also be planted in the soil of a parterre (rather than being container-grown) to add height and punctuate the design. Lower-growing herbs clipped into mounds as path edgings or to infill beds emphasize the structure of the design.

Above *Mounds of clipped box .*

Herbs for Topiary

Shrubs or trees with small leaves and a tight habit of growth make ideal subjects for topiary work.

Buxus sempervirens – Box, easy to shape, is the favourite for taller standard trees, cones, spirals and pyramids. Also comes in gold- and silver-leafed varieties.

Buxus sempervirens 'Suffruticosa' – Dwarf box is best for miniature standards and small globes.

Juniperus communis – Juniper, for tall cones and pyramids. Prune in autumn and winter to prevent bleeding of sap.

Above *An imposing display of topiary.*

J. c. 'Compressa' – A dwarf form of juniper that is suitable for lower topiary shapes.

Laurus nobilis – Bay, traditional herb-garden centrepiece as a "lollipop" or standard "mophead".

Myrtus communis – Myrtle responds well to clipping for all topiary shapes. Trim after flowering and give winter protection as it is not fully hardy.

M. c. subsp. *tarentina* – A dwarf form of myrtle ideal for compact globes and low mounds.

Rosmarinus officinalis – Rosemary, for training over wire shapes and clipping into formal hedges.

Ruta graveolens – Rue, effective clipped into mounds.

Santolina chamaecyparissus – Cotton lavender, much used in knot-garden work, also good for clipping into mounds and edges.

Satureja montana – Winter savory responds well to being clipped into low mounds or trained over a frame.

Taxus baccata – Yew, a traditional topiary tree and a favourite for hedging.

Teucrium chamaedrys – Wall germander, for knot gardens and central mounds.

Cones, Pyramids and Spheres

These are relatively simple to achieve as they require no complicated training and pruning, though it helps to have a good "eye" for the job and to stand back frequently, as you clip, to assess progress. Box is the most rewarding to work with as it produces a clean outline and is easy to shape. For a cone, start with a bushy young plant and clip it roughly to shape by eye in its first year. Feed and water it well so that it puts on new growth. In the second year, trim it into a more pronounced cone, using a tripod of canes, encircled with wires as a guide. Keep the shape by trimming twice a year in late spring and early autumn.

Above *Training rosemary over a frame.*

Wire-framed Globes

Plants with flexible stems can be trained to grow over a balloon-shaped wire frame. This works well for rosemary, curry plant (*Helichrysum italicum*), ivies, scented-leaf pelargoniums and climbers such as jasmine. Start with a young plant which has developed a reasonable length of stem. Repot it, cut out any middle growth and push the spiked end of the wire frame into the growing medium. Then tie the stems to the wire frame with twine, avoiding tight knots, which will damage the plant and impede its growth. Clip straggly stems to shape two or three times a year during the growing season.

Standards

Free-form standards: Lemon verbena (*Aloysia triphylla*) can be grown as a free-flowing standard, in contrast to formally clipped box and bay. It is more appropriate in an informal scheme where height and a structural element are required.

Select a young plant with a strong central leader. Remove any competing leaders and strong side stems, leaving higher shoots and some lower laterals to provide food, but shortening the lower laterals by half. Stake the stem to keep it straight. As the plant grows, the shortened laterals can be removed to leave a bare stem. As top laterals develop, pinch out the tips to encourage bushiness. When the plant has reached the desired height and developed a thick head of foliage, pinch out the leading shoot.

Rose standards: Old-fashioned roses trained as weeping standards make a romantic focal point in any scheme and lend colour and contrast to the strict pattern of a potager. Train them over a plastic-covered metal frame shaped like an umbrella for a more formal effect.

Aftercare

Topiary trees in containers all need regular watering and feeding throughout the whole summer to keep them healthy and growing actively. The roots of pot-grown plants are more vulnerable in cold weather than those grown in the soil, so wrap them in hessian (burlap) during frosty spells if they are hardy plants and if less than hardy move them to the protection of a cold greenhouse. Myrtle, bay, rosemary and lemon verbena are all best kept under cover during the winter months.

A mophead bay with a twisted stem

This shows how to make a standard bay with a twisted stem. For a version with a straight stem, simply cut off all side growth to leave one strong central leader, instead of three. Feed regularly throughout the growing season. Replace the top 5 cm (2 in) with fresh compost (soil mix) annually.

> ### YOU WILL NEED
> Large pot; multipurpose compost (soil mix); coarse grit (gravel); fertilizer granules; watering can; bay tree; secateurs (pruners); ratchet secateurs or pruning saw

1 *Fill a pot with free-draining, multipurpose growing compost (soil mix), and add a few handfuls of grit (gravel) and a handful of slow release fertilizer.*

2 *Repot a sturdy bay tree with plenty of straight, flexible growth. Clip off side growth to leave three straight stems.*

3 *Using ratchet secateurs or a pruning saw remove lower shoots up to about two-thirds of the overall height.*

4 *Bend over the stems, twisting them carefully, to form a plait.*

5 *Clip the crown to your preferred shape during subsequent years with secateurs (pruners).*

Pests and Diseases

Herbs in general do not suffer greatly from pests and diseases. As predominantly wild plants, they have health and vigour and many are highly aromatic, which gives them inherent protection from insects, which do not like the strong smell. But bacterial and fungal diseases do occasionally strike and no garden is without its share of insect pests. They are, after all, part of a chain, providing food for predators: hedgehogs, birds, mice and other insects.

Pests

Aphids: Blackfly and greenfly, which suck the sap of a plant, weakening it, checking growth and often transmitting viral diseases. Greenfly are attracted to roses and the various species of black aphid to the new soft growth of many green plants. Encourage natural predators such as ladybirds (ladybugs), spray with soapy water, hose with plain water, or spray with derris dust or rotenone. (Black aphids, commonly known as blackfly, should not be confused with American bloodsucking black flies, which are a true fly, rather than an aphid.)

Whitefly: These are small winged insects which usually live on brassicas but can be a problem in the greenhouse. Spray with soft soap, hang up sticky traps (yellow attracts whitefly) or introduce *Encarsia formosa*, a parasitic wasp.

Above *Damage from red spider mites.*

Red spider mite: Flourishes in hot, dry conditions, especially the greenhouse in summer. Difficult to detect without a magnifying glass – watch for bronzed or withered leaves and a fine cobweb mesh on the plants. Cut off badly affected leaves, hose off with plenty of water and spray with soft soap, or introduce a biological predator, another even smaller mite *Phytoseiulus persimilis*.

Scale insects: Flat, brownish insects which attach themselves to the undersides of leaves, suck the sap and spread a sticky substance, followed by a sooty mould. Bay is especially prone to attack. Cut off affected leaves and burn them, spray with insecticidal soap or introduce predatory wasp, *Metaphycus helvolus*, as a control.

Slugs: These do most damage in early spring and appear in the evenings. Pick them off by hand or sink jars filled with beer into the soil to attract and trap them.

Top *Scale insect on a bay leaf.*

Above *The damage caused by a scale insect.*

Diseases

Powdery mildew: A fungal disease which thrives in high humidity. Bergamot, *Monarda didyma*, is prone to it. Don't overwater or overfertilize plants. Spray with Bordeaux mixture.

Botrytis: A fungus which attacks many plants, especially if grown under glass, including tomatoes, strawberries, roses and sunflowers. Seen as a grey mould, it thrives in high humidity. Spray with Bordeaux mixture, following the manufacturer's instructions.

Rust: Brownish-red pustules appear on the leaves and the plant wilts. It affects mint. Dig up and destroy plants if severely affected. Dust with a proprietary sulphur powder following manufacturer's instructions.

Damping-off disease: A fungal disease, it affects seedlings grown under glass. Prevention is best – sow seeds thinly, as overcrowding will encourage the condition, do not overwater, and provide adequate ventilation.

Above *Greenfly suck the sap of a rose.*

Above *Caterpillars on* Polygonatum odoratum.

Prevention

Healthy plants depend on good gardening practice. They should not be overcrowded, which deprives them of light and air. Keep them free of weeds and prune regularly – always using clean secateurs (pruners) and other cutting tools so that you do not pass diseases from one plant to another by mistake.

Vigilance is important – try to remove insect infestations before they build up, and cut out diseased leaves as soon as you see them and burn them. Overfeeding plants with chemical fertilizers will only weaken them and make for fresh, sappy growth which attracts insect pests, but an organic seaweed fertilizer, applied as a spray, helps to build up their resistance.

Correct watering, especially for greenhouse and indoor plants, is also a vital factor. Overwatering tends to lead to rotting plants and inadequate ventilation encourages mildews and botrytis.

Beneficial Insects

Lacewings, ladybirds (ladybugs) and the larvae of the hoverfly all prey on aphids. Grow plants to attract them.

Lacewings: These are attracted by yarrow (*Achillea millefolium*), golden rod (*Solidago virgaurea*) and chamomile (*Chamaemelum nobile*).

Ladybirds (ladybugs): These are attracted by yarrow (*Achillea millefolium*) and pot marigolds (*Calendula officinalis*).

Hoverflies: These are attracted by yarrow (*Achillea millefolium*), lovage (*Levisticum officinale*), dill (*Anethum graveolens*), sweet cicely (*Myrrhis odorata*), fennel (*Foeniculum officinale*), golden rod (*Solidago virgaurea*) and centaury (*Centaurium erythraea*).

Other insects which prey on specific pests can be bought in.

Encarsia formosa: Small parasitic wasps that control whitefly infestations.

Phytoseiulus persimilis: A Chilean mite smaller than its red spider mite prey.

Metaphycus helvolus: Predatory wasp for scale insects.

Aphidoletes aphidimyza: A parasitic midge which preys on aphids.

Above *Yellow sticky traps used for catching whitefly in a commercial greenhouse.*

Organic Pesticides

Sometimes sprays are the only way to control a situation. But the problem with chemical sprays is that they destroy all the beneficial insects as well as pests. They also upset the balance of nature as the predatory insects are less numerous, multiply less enthusiastically than their prey and do not recover. Therefore, the next generation of pests multiplies unchecked and the problem is compounded.

It is best to use organic sprays where possible, but the most effective of these destroy insects, not just pests.

Soap is the least harmful method. A household liquid soap is suitable. Horticultural insecticidal soaps are even more effective. Derris is made from a tropical plant, and available in liquid or powder form. It kills beneficial insects as well as pests so use with great discretion. Bordeaux mixture is an inorganic chemical fungicide, but not harmful to human or animal life.

Companion Planting

The insect-repellent properties of many herbs, owing to the high concentration of aromatic oils they contain, makes them ideal companions for protecting vulnerable plants such as roses, fruit and vegetables from insect attack. Plant them in a potager garden. Rue (*Ruta graveolens*), cotton lavender (*Santolina chamaecyparissus*), curry plant (*Helichrysum angustifolia*), tansy (*Tanacetum vulgare*) and southernwood (*Artemisia abrotanum*) are all strongly aromatic and can discourage many types of pests.

Chives and garlic are beneficial to roses. They give off an odour which discourages aphids and may help cut the incidence of the disease, blackspot.

Chamomile, once known as "the plants' physician", has a reputation for improving the health and vigour of those plants and herbs surrounding it.

Pennyroyal (*Mentha pulegium*) helps to keep ants away, planted among paving. Summer savory (*Satureja hortensis*), planted in rows next to broad beans (fava beans), provides some protection from blackfly.

French marigolds, *Tagetes*, are excellent at discouraging whitefly, especially in the greenhouse.

Nicotiana sylvestris works on a trap principle. It attracts whitefly, which are then caught by the sticky stems and leaves and can be disposed of.

Using Herbs

This chapter covers when and how to harvest your herbs, with guidelines on successful drying and storing for culinary and other uses. There are suggestions for different ways of preserving herbs in oil and vinegar, sugar and honey, in medicinal tinctures or by freezing them. There is a short section on essential oils; what they are and how they are produced, their history and current uses, with some practical suggestions for making the most of them.

Above *Aromatic resins, frankincense and benzoin from the styrax tree.*

Left *Dried herbs, pot marigold and lemon verbena, with cocoa butter (at centre) and other ingredients for making herbal preparations.*

Harvesting Herbs

Harvesting the herbs you have grown is a continuous process rather than a one-off annual event. Once established, most will grow strongly enough to allow plenty of repeat picking, which in itself encourages new growth in healthy, well-cared-for plants. It makes sense not to denude small, immature plants before they have much foliage, but many annuals and herbaceous perennials, such as lovage (*Levisticum officinale*), will produce a second crop once they have flowered, if they are cut back almost to the ground. When cutting perennial, shrubby herbs think of it as pruning and aim to improve the overall shape of the plant.

The optimum time for harvesting plant material to preserve it for later use depends on the growth pattern of the individual herb and the part of it that is required – leaf, flower, seed or root.

Usually it will be during the growing season, but a few herbs, such as thyme, rosemary and sage, may be lightly picked when dormant, although they will not have such a full flavour. Whether harvesting herbs to dry for culinary use, cosmetics and pot-pourri or for home remedies, the following guidelines will ensure good results:

• Choose a fine, sunny day for picking, so that the essential oil content, which gives the plant its flavour and scent, is at its best. Wait until any dew or residual raindrops have evaporated – herbs tend to go mouldy before the drying process is complete if picked when wet – but try to finish in the morning before volatile oils have been drawn to the surface by the heat and dissipated.

• Use only sharp scissors or secateurs (pruners) so as not to damage the plant and limit further cropping. Make sure that your equipment is clean and that sticky blades do not pass pest or disease problems from one plant to another.

• Pick only prime material from plants that are at their peak – avoid anything damaged, discoloured, diseased or spent with age.

• Pick herbs in small quantities, only as much as you can deal with at one time. Herbs should not be left in heaps, waiting to be processed, as even quite a small pile encourages heat and deterioration sets in. The idea is to preserve the plant before the active constituents start to break down and lose viability.

• Flowers and foliage must be wiped clean and be insect free before they are processed: they can be lightly sponged and patted dry with a paper towel, but do not try to wash them as this will impede drying.

Above *Cutting a head of angelica to collect the seeds.*

Left *A freshly gathered harvest of garden herbs, ready to be preserved and stored in containers for future use.*

Leaves: Most should be picked before they come into flower, when leaf flavour and texture are at their best. Pick small-leafed plants on the stem for stripping later – larger leaves may be picked individually. Shrubby perennials which last through the winter should not be cut severely late in the season, as this will weaken them and leave them vulnerable to frost damage.

Flowers: These should be cut soon after they have opened when they are at their best, and not left to drop their petals, when colour and scent will be minimal. Pick single blooms or flower heads as appropriate and strip off petals or florets when spreading them to dry. Lavender should be picked with a long stem, and flowers such as borage, where only the tiny blue "star" is required, need careful individual collection.

Seeds: The pods or seed heads must be picked as soon as they are ripe, when they are no longer green, but before they fall. This means watching them carefully, as they can ripen and disperse very quickly.

Roots and rhizomes: These are usually collected during their dormant period in autumn or winter. When digging them up, try to leave some portion of the root so that the plant can regenerate. With some herbs, such as horseradish, this is not difficult, as it will regrow vigorously from the tiniest portion of root. Wash roots and rhizomes thoroughly with plenty of cold water and cut into pieces before processing.

Bulbs: These include garlic and onions. Dig them up in late summer to early autumn.

Bark: Bark should not be stripped from very young trees. They must never be ring-barked (stripped of bark all round the circumference of the trunk), nor should too much be taken in one year as this could kill the tree. Tools should be clean and sharp, and the lowest cut made at 1 m (3 ft) above ground level. Endangered or protected species should not be harvested at all.

Wild plants: Wild plants should be picked with the utmost caution, both for safety reasons and for the sake of the environment. Many wild plants are protected by law (check if this applies), and should not be touched – in any case none should be uprooted or overpicked, especially if less than common. Any that grow near crops should be treated with suspicion, as they may contain pesticide residues, and of course you must be confident of correct identification. If you are not sure, leave them alone.

Right *Fresh sage leaves tied up in small bunches for drying.*

Harvesting marjoram

1 *Cut bunches of healthy material at mid-morning on a dry day.*

2 *Strip off the lower leaves, which may otherwise become damaged.*

3 *Twist an elastic (rubber) band around the stems to hold them tightly together.*

4 *Gather as many bunches as you need, then the bunches can be hung in a dry, well-ventilated place where they are protected from light.*

Drying

Successful drying depends on removing the moisture in the fresh material without sacrificing the volatile oil content. The process has to be completed quickly so that oils are not lost through a natural process of decay, but not so quickly that they are destroyed by heat. The key to success is the right temperature and low humidity.

An average temperature for commercially dried herbs is 38°C (99°F), but this would be difficult to provide at home without special equipment. Between 20–32°C (68–90°F) works well and can be found in an airing cupboard, or a cupboard near a hot-water heater. A spare room, with an electric heater (not directed straight at petals or loose material), could also be used.

The place chosen should be dry and well ventilated (garages are not really suitable, but a clean shed may be ideal) and, for better colour preservation, dark. Sun drying is a traditional method in climates where air temperatures are high and humidity low, but it does lead to colour loss and there is also a greater risk of contamination than in an indoor, controlled environment.

Oven drying is generally too fierce for flowers and foliage, even at its lowest setting, but it is suitable for roots. Microwaving is not ideal as it is necessary to include a small container of water to prevent arcing, and this makes for humidity, which is counterproductive.

Green Herbs

Small-leaved green herbs may be dried on the stem and larger leaves dried individually. Spread them on slatted trays, or on fine netting stretched over a frame so that air can circulate beneath, and put them in a warm, dark place with some ventilation.

Leave the herbs until they are crackly dry to the touch. The length of time will depend on the thickness and moisture content of the leaf, the level of heat provided and humidity in the air. The process takes from 3–4 days to a week at the most. Once dried, strip leaves off the stems, or crumble larger ones into small pieces ready to store. Wearing cotton gloves makes the job easier on the hands.

Herbs may also be tied in bunches with raffia or string and hung up in a clean, airy place to dry.

Above *Drying lavender commercially on a custom-built, movable frame.*

Flowers

Twist off heads of large blooms, such as roses, and spread out the petals on paper on slatted trays. Put in a warm place and leave them until papery dry.

Pot marigold (*Calendula officinalis*) flowers are easier to dry whole, then twist off the petals afterwards if required.

Lavender is best hung up in bunches, tied loosely with string or raffia, and with the heads in paper bags to exclude dust and catch petals that may fall as they dry.

Once the flowers are dried, they may be left whole, according to their intended use, or stripped from the stems in the same way as green herbs.

Chive flowers, or rosebuds that are required for decorative purposes, will keep a good shape if dried upright, with stems pushed through wire cake trays.

Specially treated dry sand or silica gel may also be used for drying flowers, resulting in a good colour and perfect shape. Place a flower on a thin layer of sand, sift more sand gently over it until covered and leave for three weeks in a warm, dry place. Uncover carefully.

Above *Herbs drying in a dark, clean and well-ventilated shed.*

Above *Lavender, tied in bunches for drying, is well spaced to allow air to circulate.*

Seeds

A good way to dry seeds is to pick the seed heads with stems attached. Tie them in bunches, insert the heads into paper bags and hang them up in a warm, airy place. When completely dry, clean off the pods or husks before storing in clearly marked envelopes. Seeds should not be stored in polythene (plastic), which encourages moisture.

Roots

Roots require a higher temperature than flowers and leaves for successful drying from 50–60°C (120–140°F). An oven, at a very low setting, with the door left open is suitable. Make sure the roots are scrubbed clean, then cut them in pieces and spread on baking trays. Put them in a cool oven and turn at intervals to ensure even heat. Leave until brittle, but test frequently as they should not become shrivelled and overbrown – length of time depends on the size and moisture content of root pieces.

Storing

Dried herbs and flowers deteriorate quickly, losing aroma and colour, if left exposed to light and air. Always store them in the dark and keep in a dry place. Flowers and foliage required for pot-pourri can be kept in paper bags, airtight tins or glass jars.

Above *Dried herbs retain colour and flavour when stored in opaque containers.*

Above *Dried bay leaves in a jar.*

Right *Pot-pourri ingredients, stored in glass, are best kept in a dark cupboard.*

Preserving

Preserving the flavour and perfume of herbs in vegetable oils or in vinegar is easy to do and these have many uses in culinary and cosmetic recipes or in home remedies. A mixed-herb oil, or one with a single flavour, such as basil, adds interest to salad dressings, stir-fries, pizza and pasta dishes, grilled or barbecued meat, fish or vegetables. Rosemary oil is the ideal ingredient for bath lotions and beauty treatments and oil infused with garlic makes an effective liniment for relieving aches and pains.

Above *Finish off oil bottles by neatly winding cotton string around waxed paper and then tying it securely with a reef knot.*

Tips for success:

• Use a good-quality, mild-flavoured oil, such as sunflower or safflower, so that the taste of the oil doesn't compete with the flavour of the herbs. Extra-virgin olive oil, which has a strong flavour of its own, is not suitable.

• Always cover herbs completely with oil during the infusing process. Any bits left sticking out will start to deteriorate and affect the quality of the oil.

• It is important to remove the plant material before storage. If left it will start to decay and the oil will become cloudy and sour.

To make herb oil

1 *Put a good handful of herbs or flower heads into a clean glass jar – either a single herb, such as marjoram used here, or a mixture, such as oregano, rosemary and thyme – and crush them lightly to release the essential oils.*

2 *Pour in a mild vegetable oil until the herbs (or flowers) are completely covered, otherwise any that are not covered will go mouldy. Cover the jar and stand it in a warm place – a sunny windowsill is fine.*

3 *After about a week, strain off the herbs, replace with fresh ones and leave to infuse for a further week. This process can be repeated until the flavour is strong enough.*

4 *Remove the herbs and pour the oil into a clean, sterilized bottle with an airtight lid. The oil will keep for a few weeks if extra flowers have been added, or 6 months without extra flowers.*

YOU WILL NEED
A handful of fresh herbs or about
12 flower-heads; 400 ml/³⁄₄pt
light vegetable oil; jar with top;
filter

Herb Vinegars

Herb vinegar is made in the same way as a herb oil. A great variety of flavouring materials can be used: fresh or dried leaves, spices, chillies, garlic, fruit or flower petals. Tarragon vinegar is a classic for salad dressing. Fruit and flower flavours, such as raspberry, blackberry, lavender or rose petal, add sharpness to sweet dishes and are useful as home remedies. Raspberry vinegar helps to ease a sore throat, and lavender, applied as a compress, may relieve a headache.

Some herb vinegars can be used as antiseptics for cleaning surfaces or as poultices; some can be dabbed on the skin to counteract a range of conditions; others can be taken internally as a tonic or prophylactic.

An excellent ingredient for home-made cosmetics is cider vinegar; it restores the acid mantle of the skin and is a traditional ingredient in skin lotions and hair rinses. Use it to make a mint-and-marigold or rose petal vinegar, which is then diluted – two or three tablespoons in a basin of water – to splash over the face as a general toner.

To make herb vinegar: Fill a clean jar to about one-third with herb leaves, spices, fruit or flowers of your choice, top up with cider vinegar and leave to infuse for two or three weeks. It is not usually necessary to use more than one batch of herbs or other flavouring ingredient to obtain a strong enough flavour, as it is for oil.

Vinegar is a better preservative than oil, so it is possible to leave in some of the herb used, such as a sprig of tarragon, for decorative effect, but always replace the infused material with a fresh piece. Dried material can be left in vinegar indefinitely. Coloured peppercorns, rosemary, chillies and dried bay leaves look most attractive when left in a spiced vinegar.

Above *Fresh herbs add a spicy, aromatic flavour to vinegar. Clockwise from front, rosemary, sage and marjoram.*

Right *Tarragon (left) and a mixed herb vinegar with bay leaves.*

Preserving in Sugar

Sugar makes an excellent preservative and was a traditional method of retaining the properties of herbs and flowers. Old herbal manuscripts are full of recipes for herbal syrups and conserves made with sugar, or more often, honey.

Above *Sugar flavoured with lavender flowers is ideal for baking.*

Lavender sugar: This is a delicious way to impart a subtle fragrance to cakes, biscuits, meringues and other sweet dishes, without the coarse texture of the whole petals. To make lavender sugar, bruise dried lavender flowers, stripped from the stem, and add them to caster (superfine) or icing (confectioner's) sugar before storing in an airtight jar until required. Sieve out the flowers before use. Ten to 15 heads of lavender will be enough to lend fragrance to 450g (1 lb) of sugar.

Crystallized petals: Many edible flowers may be used for this purpose. To make the petals: Check the petals are dry, clean and insect-free. Spread them on a greaseproof-paper covered baking tray. Then paint them, using a fine artist's brush, with a thin coat of lightly whipped egg white (just broken up, rather than frothy), and sprinkle thickly with caster (superfine) sugar. Put in the bottom of a very low oven with the door left open, until completely dry and brittle, but not brown.

Top *Crystallized violas make delicate decorations for cakes and sweets.*

Above *Lavender honey is easy to make and has a subtly distinctive flavour.*

Herb honey: The finest honeys are those which are made by bees collecting from a single flower source such as lime blossom or thyme. Both honey from the hive and many herbs, such as rosemary and garlic, have antiseptic properties. In combination they are helpful for soothing sore throats and cold or flu symptoms, taken in teaspoonfuls. They can also be used as a sweetener for herb teas.

To make herb honey: Put a small handful of herbs, such as rosemary, thyme or lavender flowers, into a saucepan. Bruise with a wooden spoon, add the contents of a 225 g (8 oz) jar of honey and heat gently until melted but not boiling. Leave to infuse for about one hour before straining the mixture. Discard the herbs and pour the honey into a jar with an airtight lid for storage.

Freezing Herbs

A convenient way to preserve fresh herbs for later use is to freeze them in ice cubes for adding to soups, stews and other cooked dishes. Simply chop them finely, put into ice-cube trays and top up with water before freezing. Whole mint leaves or borage flowers may be frozen in the same way for floating in drinks.

Culinary herbs, stripped from the stems but not chopped, can be frozen packed in polythene (plastic) bags, or cartons, for short periods of time. They will not, of course, have the texture of fresh leaves once thawed. This is a useful method of preserving herbs that do not keep a good aroma when dried, such as basil, parsley, chives and mint.

Tinctures

Many herbs may be preserved in alcohol for medicinal use. They are best made as a cold infusion using dried herbs and alcohol with little flavour of its own, such as vodka. This makes a potent preparation, as the essential oils and active constituents of many herbs are soluble in alcohol. It should be taken in small doses of drops, or teaspoons, and, it is strongly suggested, as directed by a qualified practitioner.

To make a tincture: Put dried herbs in a jar and top up with a mixture of one part of water to two parts of vodka. As a general guideline, 15 g (½oz) of dried herbs to 300 ml (½ pint/⅔ cup) of alcohol and water mixed are standard quantities. Seal the jar and leave in a warm, dark place for one week, after which time the active constituents will have been extracted and the herbs will start to deteriorate. Strain out the herbs and rebottle.

Left *From left to right: lavender, violet leaf and juniper tinctures.*

Making herb ice cubes

1 *Pick some mint leaves, selecting small undamaged ones, and strip them from the stem.*

2 *Put a single leaf into each compartment of an ice-cube tray, top up with water and freeze.*

Above *Edible flowers and herb leaves make unusual ice cubes for floating in drinks.*

Herbal Essential Oils

What are essential oils? The essential, or volatile, oil in a plant gives it its scent. Despite the name, essential oils are not oily – a drop applied to paper does not usually leave any mark. They are volatile liquids, which evaporate at normal air temperatures and are secreted from minute glands and hairs in the leaves, stems, flowers, seeds, fruit, roots or bark of plants and trees.

Some plants, such as roses, contain their essential oil mainly in the flowers; others, such as lemon balm (*Melissa officinalis*), mainly in the leaves. The orange tree (*Citrus aurantium*) contains three differently named essential oils, in the flowers (neroli), the leaves (petitgrain) and the rind of the fruit (orange oil).

The organic chemical structure of plant essential oils is extremely complex. Analysis by gas liquid chromatography (GLC) reveals that peppermint oil, whose 50 per cent menthol content provides its minty smell, has 98 other constituents. Flower essential oils have as many as several hundred components. For this reason it is impossible to chemically reproduce an exact copy of a naturally occurring essential oil in the laboratory.

Above *The leaves of* Melissa officinalis *are distilled to produce a cheering, tonic essential oil.*

Above right *Essential oils have long been valued for their therapeutic properties.*

Production

Essential oils are soluble in fats, vegetable and mineral oils and in alcohol. For the most part they do not dissolve in water, though some of their constituents may do so. The main fragrance molecules of roses and orange flowers, for example, are soluble in water. Steam distillation is the most frequent method of extraction, and volatile solvents and alcohol are sometimes used in the process. A few fragile flower fragrances are still obtained by the centuries-old method of macerating the petals in trays of fat, and volatile oil from orange rind is extracted by expression: that is by pressing it out, nowadays by machine, but formerly pressed by hand. Quality is affected by varying soils, climates and harvesting conditions. Some oils may have been diluted or adulterated. It is not easy to tell, so look for a reliable source.

Using Essential Oils

Plant essential oils and extracts are widely used in the pharmaceutical, cosmetic and food industries. In the home they are used therapeutically in aromatherapy and herbal medicine, by taking them internally, by inhaling them in vaporizers and in fragrance products such as pot-pourri, by massaging them into the skin, by applying them in compresses, or by putting them in the bath. They are sometimes used in a domestic context to flavour food, but only in very small quantities, the whole plant being safer and usually more satisfactory for culinary use.

The important thing to remember is that, as extracts of the active principles of plants, essential oils are concentrated substances and should be taken internally only in controlled, drop-sized doses. When applied externally they must be diluted in a carrier oil.

Essential Oils in History

Essential oils take their name from the *quinta essentia*, or quintessence, a term coined by a Swiss physician Paracelsus, 1493–1541. He took the medieval theory of alchemy, which sought to isolate the *prima materia*, or elemental matter, of a substance, and applied it specifically to plants. His goal was to divide the "essential matter" of a plant from its "non-essential" components.

In ancient times, extracting plant fragrance by macerating it in oil or fat was common, and a technique of destructive distillation, such as that which produces oil of turpentine, was also known. At the beginning of the 11th century, steam distillation as a means of making plant-scented waters was discovered, usually credited to the physician, Avicenna, 980–1037, author of the *Canon of Medicine*. Arnald de Villanova, d. 1311, a Spanish doctor, further popularized the use of distilled herb waters for medicinal purposes.

Distillation was seen at the time as a means of refining plant material to its purest form, through fire, and alcohol was widely used in the process as producing the best results. But it was not until the mid-16th century that the nature of essential oils was understood and the process of separating them from the distillate put into practice.

By the beginning of the 17th century plant essential oils were available from professional pharmacies, as well as being produced on a domestic scale in the stillrooms of grand houses. Many herbals and old recipe books contained detailed instructions.

Inhaling Essential Oils

Breathing in the fragrance of essential oils has an immediate effect on mood and can be immensely therapeutic. An essential oil burner or vaporizer is one of the best ways to do this. You could also put a few drops of oil on a handkerchief to tuck under a pillow, or mix some into a pot-pourri of flowers and herbs.

To lift depression, anxiety and nervous tension try essential oil of frankincense, jasmine, neroli, rose or sandalwood. Sedative oils for insomnia include chamomile, juniper, lavender and marjoram. For stress and shock there is cedarwood, melissa or peppermint, and for mental fatigue and lethargy use basil, black pepper, cardamom or pine.

Bath Oils

Adding essential oil in drops to the bath water is another way to benefit from the fragrance. To make a bath oil for dry skins, mix about 20 drops of essential oil into a 10 ml (2 tsp) bottle of almond or sunflower oil which has first been infused with fresh flowers or herbs, such as chamomile or lavender.

A lavender bath is deeply relaxing, mildly antiseptic and helps to heal tiny cuts and scratches, bites or swellings. It is also soothing when you have a cold.

Right *A bath oil including essential oil of chamomile is soothing to sensitive skins.*

Below *Lavender, mixed with a light oil for massage, releases an aroma which will help ease stress headaches and promote calm and restful sleep. It also helps muscular aches and pains. To release the scent, warm the oil slightly before you begin.*

Insect Repellent Oils

Essential oil of lavender makes an effective insect repellent. Good quality and pure lavender and tea-tree oils are two of the few oils that may be applied directly to the skin. But if you are not sure of its provenance, or are likely to suffer from allergies, dilute it in a carrier (such as sunflower) oil first. Candles scented with citronella or eucalyptus help deter midges and flying insects.

Sources and suppliers

UNITED KINGDOM

SUPPLIERS OF ESSENTIAL OILS

Culpeper Ltd
Hadstock Road
Linton
Cambridge CB1 6NJ
Tel 01223 891196

The Fragrant Earth Co. Ltd
PO Box 182
Taunton
Somerset TA1 1YR
Tel 01458 831216 for mail order catalogue.

Neal's Yard Remedies
29 John Dalton Street
Manchester M2 6DS
Tel 0161 831 7875 for mail order catalogue.

Shirley Price
Essentia House
Upper Bond Street
Hinckley
Leicestershire LE10 1RS
Tel 01455 615466 for mail order catalogue.

MEDICINAL AND CULINARY HERBS

G. Baldwin & Co.
171–173 Walworth Road
London SE17 1RN
Tel 020 7703 5550

Potters Herbal Supplies
Leyland Mill Lane
Lancashire WN1 2SB
Tel 01942 405100 for mail order cut herbs.

Poyntzfield Herb Nursery
Black Isle by Dingwall
Ross & Cromarty
IV7 8LX
Tel 01381 610352 for mail order plants.
Informative catalogue sent on receipt of four
first class stamps.

Rosemary Titterington
Iden Croft Herbs
Frittenden Road
Kent TN12 0DH
Tel 01580 891432 for mail order.

NORTH AMERICA

SUPPLIERS OF ESSENTIAL OILS

The Body Shop
2870 Janitell Road
Colorado Springs, CO 80906
Tel (800) 263-9746

Lorann Oils
P.O. Box 22009
Lansing, MI 48909–2009
Tel (800) 248-1302 for mail order.

Above left *Golden feverfew.*

Below *A deeply coloured knot garden.*

MEDICINAL AND CULINARY HERBS

Caprilands Herb Farm
Silver Street
North Coventry, CT 06238

Richter's Herbs
Goodwood
Ontario
Canada LOC 1AO
Tel (905) 640-6677

Seeds Blum
HC 33 Box 2057
Boise, ID 83706
Tel (208) 342-0858
Order tel (800) 538-3658

AUSTRALIA

MEDICINAL AND CULINARY HERBS

Bundanoon Village Nursery
71 Penrose Road
Bundanoon 2578
NSW
Tel (02) 4883-6303
e-mail: cabbage@pbq.com.au. A nursery in a
garden. Classes on use of herbs, seeds and
some Chinese medicinal herb tubers available
by mail order.

Above Helianthus annuus.

Above Monarda didyma *'Cambridge Scarlet'.*

Above *Wild strawberry and marjoram pot.*

Chamomile Farm
79 Monbulk Road
Emerald 3782
Victoria
Tel (03) 5968-4807. No mail order.

Darling Mills Farm
62 Francis Street
Castle Hill 2154
NSW
Tel (02) 9634-2843
Fax (02) 9894-7439
Wide variety of salad leaves and the more
common herbs as well as some Asian herbs.

Herbie's Spices
745 Darling Street
Rozelle 2039
NSW
Tel (02) 9555-6035
Website:http://www.herbies.com.au
All culinary herbs and spices in one place.
Huge range. Mail order for dried herbs
nationally and throughout the Pacific.

House of Herbs
1 Digney Street
Sandy Bay
Tasmania 7005
Tel (03) 6224-3788. Wide range to show size
and shape under Tasmanian conditions.

Right Tanacetum cinerariifolium.

Lillydale Herb Farm
Mangans Road
Lilydale 3140
Victoria
Tel (03) 9735-0486
Display gardens with medicinal, culinary,
fragrant, companion and insect repellent
plants. Shop with range of herbal items
and books.

Renaissance Herbs
Lot 521
Hakone Road
Warnervale 2259
Tel (02) 4392-4600
Fax (02) 4393-1221
Largest range – supplies to nurseries
nationally through franchised growers
throughout Australia.

TLC Herbs
Lot 10
Old Coach Road
Aldinga 5173 SA
Tel (08) 8577-7161
Many varieties, including more unusual ones.
Mail order.

Resource information

For information on any aspect of the herb
industry in Australia, the *Australian Herb
Industry Resource Guide* by Kim Fletcher is
invaluable. Regularly updated. Available from:

Focus on Herbs
Consultancy & Information Service
PO Box 203, Launceston
Tasmania 7250

Index

Page numbers in *italics* refer to illustrations.

The publisher would like to thank the following people for assisting with the photography for this book:

Roger and Linda Bastin
Kruidenkwekerij Herb Nursery
Trichterweg 148a
6446 AT Brunssum
Holland

Christine and Peter Bench and Mrs
  Nancy Bench
The Herb Nursery
Thistleton
Oakham
Rutland LE15 7RE
Tel 01572 767658

Chris and Mandie Dennis
  (Proprietors)
The Citrus Centre
Marehill Nursery
West Mare Lane
Marehill
Pulborough
Sussex RH20 2EA
Tel 01798 872786

Adam Gordon
Rochfords
Joseph Rochford Gardens Ltd
Pipers End
Letty Green
Hertford SG14 2PB
Tel 01707 261370

Henry Doubleday Research
  Association
Ryton Organic Gardens
Coventry
CV8 3LG
Tel 024 7630 3517

Simon and Judith Hopkinson
  (and Anne)
Hollington Nurseries
Woolton Hill
Newbury
Berkshire RG20 9XT
Tel 01653 253908

Victoria Ker
Bedwyn Common
Wiltshire

The Kew Gardener
4a Station Approach
Kew Gardens
Surrey TW9 3QB
Tel 020 8332 9630

Anne Marie Powell
Garden Designer
West London
Tel 020 8840 1230

Letta Proper Pranger
Castle Hex
Belgium

Sally Reed
Braxton Gardens
Braxton Courtyard
Lymore Lane
Melford-on-Sea
Hampshire SO41 0TX
Tel 01590 642008

Duncan and Susan Ross
Poyntzfield Herb Nursery
Black Isle by Dingwall
Ross & Cromarty
Scotland IV7 8LX
Tel 01381 610352

The Royal Botanic Gardens
Kew
Surrey TW9 3AB
Tel 020 8332 5000

Lord Salisbury/Michael Pickard
  (Curator)
Hatfield House
Hatfield
Hertfordshire AL9 5NQ
Tel 01707 262823

Richard Scott
The Herb Farm
Peppard Road
Sonning Common
Reading
Berkshire RG4 9NJ

The Shakespeare Birthplace Trust
Shakespeare Centre
Henley Street
Stratford-upon-Avon CV37 6QW
Tel 01789 204016

The Shrewsbury Quest
Abbey Foregate
Shrewsbury
Shropshire SY2 6AH
Tel 01743 366355

Roger Souvereyns
Scholteshof Restaurant and Hotel
  with Gardens
Belgium

Phillip C Stallard
Site Facilities Officer
(Tretower Court)
CADW Welsh Historic Monuments

Peter Turner
The National Herb Centre
Banbury Road
Warmington
Near Banbury
Oxfordshire OX17 1DF
Tel 01295 690999

Stijn Vanormelingen
De Horne Restaurant and Gardens
Brugstraat 30a Vechmaal
Belgium

Susie & Kevin White
Hexham Herbs
Chesters Walled Garden
Chollerford
Hexham
Northumberland NE46 4BQ
Tel 01434 681483

AUTHOR'S ACKNOWLEDGEMENTS

My thanks to the following people for specialist information: Alan Gear of the Henry Doubleday Research Association, on the use of comfrey in the garden; Dr. Stanley Deans on thyme oil; Duncan Ross of Poyntzfield Herb Nursery on ginseng; Dr. Rosita Arvigo and the Traditional Healers Foundation of Belize, on plants of Central America; and also to Dr. Katya Svoboda of the Scottish Agricultural College, Dr. Rosemary Cole of the National Herb Centre and Dr. Charles Hill.

PICTURE CREDITS

The publisher would like to thank the following picture agencies and individuals for the permission to reproduce their pictures for use in this book:
Pages 10 bl, 14 bl, 17 tl ET Archive; pages 14 tr, 15 bl Edimedia; pages 15 tr, 16 bl, 17br, 20 bl The Bridgeman Art Library; pages 11 tr Vaughn Fleming, 20 tr Clay Perry, 26 rc David Askham, 43 br Steven Wooster – The Garden Picture Library; pages 21t, 41 br, 53 cl, 78 tr & cr, 79 Jessica Houdret; pages 21 bl, 40 bl, 41 bl Lucy Mason; pages 21 tr, 24 tr, 36 bl, 48 tr, 51 br, 59 tr Jacqui Hurst; pages 32 br Adrian Thomas, 44 bl Neil Joy, 57 Michael Jones, 60 tr Geoffrey S. Chapman – A–Z Botanical Collection Ltd; pages 34 bl, 41 tr & tl, 67, 68, 69 tl, tc, tr, 73 tr & bl, 80/81, 82 br, 85 tr, 86, 88 bc, 90 tr Michelle Garrett; pages 82 bl, 83 br, 85 br & bl, 86 cl, 88 tl & tr, 89 bl, 91 cr Polly Wreford.

key t = top, b = bottom,
c = centre, l = left, r = right

Left *A bed of mixed thymes.*

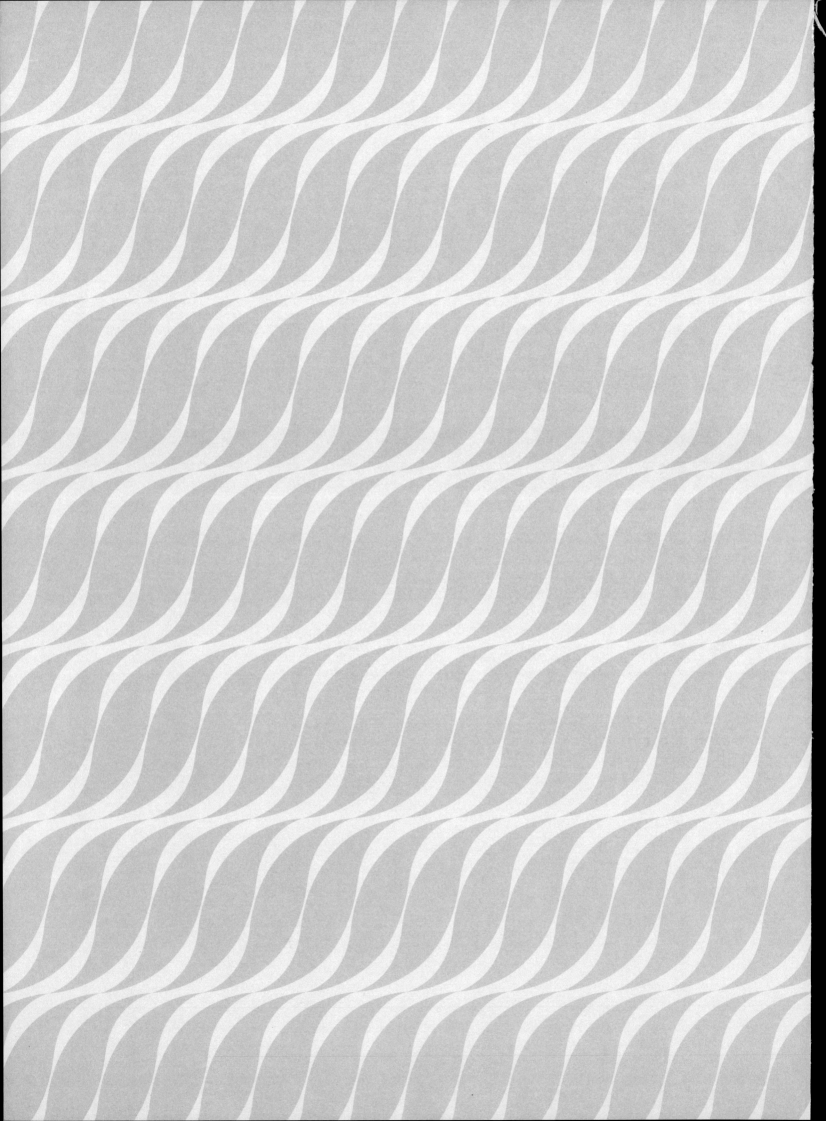